THE BLOOD

AND

THE CROSS

STEVEN GALINDO

Seven Messages on

the Precious Blood of Jesus

and the Cross of Calvary

The Blood and the Cross.

Copyright 2013 by Steven Galindo. All rights reserved. No portion of this book in whole or in part may be used without the expressed written consent of the author.

Dedication

To my friend and brother-in-Christ, Buddy Price who befriended me in my first pastorate, and exemplified the unconditional love of Jesus to my family and I during a difficult struggle.

As a father, husband, businessman, neighbor, friend, church elder, deacon and witness there are few - if any - who surpassed him.

There are some people you just know will be in Heaven waiting for you with a smile.

Buddy, I look forward to seeing yours.

Table of Contents

Introduction

1. I was the Thief on the Cross
2. When I See the Blood I will Pass Over You
3. In the Shadow of the Cross
4. When Blood Cries Out
5. It Wasn't the Cross that Killed Jesus
6. The Cry of the Centurion
7. Let Us Go and Die with Him

Conclusion
Blessing
About the Author
Other Books by Steven Galindo

THE BLOOD

AND

THE CROSS

Seven Messages

on the precious Blood of Jesus

and the Cross of Christ

INTRODUCTION

The inspiration for this book came from my wife who in a conversation with me mentioned that she had not heard many sermons on the blood or the cross like she used to hear when she was younger and new to Pentecost. I thought a moment and had to agree with her. I was a recent Christian having been saved for about thee years at the time, and I had only heard one message on the cross from a Baptist minister whose church I had visited after surrendering to God.

I thought it curious that of all the things preachers find to speak about they seem to stay away from the blood and the cross, and instead focus on feeling good, being happy and thinking positive. Or "Seven Steps to [this]" and "Four Ways to do [that]". I am not opposed to those messages. I like feeling good, being happy and I always try to stay positive. Plus, I love having two or three steps to anything. But when your entire repertoire of sermon material revolves around enjoying life and being successful, and you fail to mention the precious blood of Jesus and the cross of Calvary, you're basically focusing on the icing -- but forgetting the cake it's sitting on!

All that we have, all that we are and all that we can ever hope to be is found in Christ and what He did on the cross.

Understand the cross, and suffering in life begins to make sense.

Understand the cross, and the phrase "self-sacrifice" remakes your nature. Understand the cross – what happened there in the spirit world and how it impacts your soul through all eternity -- and you'll have a new appreciation for what that lonely Galilean did for you and me over 2,000 years ago.

The cross was made of wood. Jesus stained it red with His blood. The Father demanded a perfect sacrifice to cleanse us of our sins forever.

And according to the law almost all things are purified with blood, and without shedding of blood there is no remission. (Heb. 9:22)

There was only one who could lie there and be nailed to our shame. It was the young carpenter from Bethlehem who stood in the gap and took the punishment reserved for us. I have never had anyone take my punishment except Jesus. He paid dearly to set me free. He paid with His lifeblood. He gave every drop to make sure we could be saved, that we could be healed, that we could go free.

The blood is precious to me because of what it represents.

Yes, it is powerful and rebukes devils.
Yes, it is holy, cleansing us from our sins.
Yes, it is mighty to save the souls of the lost.
But I hear the blood of Jesus speak, and what I hear it say is: "Mercy".
God's love drove Him to the cross.
His love nailed Him to a tree.

It was love He poured out on that lonely hill. His spilt blood says to me: "I love you more than I love life itself. I freely surrender my life to purchase you for God."

"You are worthy to take the scroll, and to open its seals; for You were slain, and have redeemed us to God by Your blood out of every tribe and tongue and people and nation." (Revelation 5:9)

So I undertook to write a sermon on the blood and the cross. But one message led to two. And those two led to more. Soon the Holy Spirit poured several into me which I preached on Communion Sundays for my brothers and sisters.

I asked the Holy Spirit why He gave me these messages and not other, better preachers than myself.

As I waited, He said simply, "You asked."

I have collected the messages here and rewritten them from my sermon notes. I hope they bless you as much as they have blessed me and the people who have heard them. In researching, writing and preaching them, they changed me.

They changed my view of who I am,
They changed my view of what I am worth,
They changed my view of who He is,
and what He accomplished for me.

I know I will never be the same. I pray these life-giving words will change you forever. I hope in discovering them (or rediscovering them) that you find a newfound appreciation and become eternally grateful for the precious blood of Jesus, and that terrible -- but wonderful -- cross on Golgotha.

Steven Galindo
Joplin, Missouri
September, 2013

Chapter 1:   I was the Thief on the Cross

Luke 23:39-43

>One of the criminals who hung there hurled insults at him: "Aren't you the Christ? Save yourself and us!"
>But the other criminal rebuked him. "Don't you fear God," he said, "since you are under the same sentence? We are punished justly, for we are getting what our deeds deserve. But this man has done nothing wrong."
>Then he said, "Jesus, remember me when you come into your kingdom."
>Jesus answered him, "I tell you the truth, today you will be with me in paradise."

We tend to judge people, comparing ourselves to them and making judgments as to who is living closer to God. Isn't it funny how we always tend to see ourselves as a little bit better than those around us? Isn't it interesting how **we tend to judge others by what they say and do but we tend to judge ourselves by what we *meant* to say or by what we *meant* to do?** I find it interesting that we tend to see our mistakes as little mistakes -- little sins -- whereas our enemies seem to commit great, BIG sins.

But in the sight of God, we are all equal.

"We have all sinned and fallen short of the glory of God" (Romans 3:23).

None of us are perfect. None of us are righteous in and of ourselves. Your sins may be small and insignificant compared to others in your mind but the Bible teaches that all sin is evil in God's sight. He doesn't rate sins the way we do. God sees sin as sin. There aren't any little white ones or big black ones. They are all wrong and need to be repented of.

Take into consideration all the wrong things you've done, all the wrong things you've said and all the wrong thoughts you've considered. Now add them up across your entire lifetime. Now multiply them times every person in the world, and throw in all people everywhere since mankind was created. When you look at it like that, you have to admit we're a sinful people. Fortunately for us, we're made by a loving, forgiving God.

Looking at life that way, we must confess: **we are marvelous examples of God's grace and mercy.**

We are all thieves. We steal time and talents. We steal tithes and offerings. We steal our lives away from God and do with them what we want. We're thieves. Our actions speak for themselves. We've been caught red-handed. There's no denying it. You can say what you want. Make any excuse you can find. The bottom line is: we are all thieves.

The root of thievery is selfishness. One man has what another wants. The second man can't seem to earn it or keep his own so what does he do? He steals it from the first man, of course.

"Take what you want. If you get caught you can make excuses later."

"If you need it, take it. They won't know it's gone till tomorrow."

"If you must have it, steal it. They would do the same if they could."

Don't worry about the fact that the other person may have worked hard for it and earned it. That doesn't matter. What matters is your personal happiness. If you're satisfied, then everything is justified.

That's selfishness! That's thievery!

The Bible says we are thieves when we don't give our tithes and offerings.

Will a man rob God? Yet you rob me. But you ask, "How do we rob you?" In tithes and offerings. You are under a curse—the whole nation of you—because you are robbing me. (Malachi 3:8-9)

When we choose to keep that which belongs to God, we are stealing from Him. That's selfish. We make excuses. We say: "I can't afford to give anything to God."

Let me tell you, **you can't afford NOT to.**

We use a talent or gift God has given us to make ourselves wealthy but we don't acknowledge the glory belongs to the Lord. That's selfish. We want the glory. We want the fame. We want the recognition.

Consider this: **everything we do well is because the Lord gave us the ability to do it well!**

We are thieves of time. There are so many times when we could be doing something to bless other people. Instead, what are we doing? We spend it on ourselves. We plan our day, schedule what must be done and what we want to do. Do we give a thought to how the Lord would have us plan our day? Do we take into consideration how much time we are going to give Him? Maybe He wants us to go and bless someone else instead of sitting around waiting to be blessed. When we do what we want to do with our time instead of asking Him what He would have us do, that's selfish. We're stealing time for ourselves that could be spent ministering to someone else.

Now please hear me: I am not suggesting we should spend *all* of our time on others. There is a time for every minister of the Lord to withdraw and relax. Even Jesus withdrew from the crowds who wanted ministry.

But Jesus often withdrew to lonely places and prayed. (Luke 5:16)

Jesus withdrew with his disciples to the lake, and a large crowd from Galilee followed. (Mark 3:7)

Far too often we spend more time taking care of us -- and seeing to our needs -- instead of taking care of the Lord and seeing to *His* needs. His needs frequently require us to sacrifice and give up time (we want to indulge ourselves in), and spend it with others, being a blessing to them.

We take this mortal life that God has given us, and we do what we want with it. I have heard people say – and I have said it myself: "This is *my* life. I am going to do what I want to do, and I don't care what anyone thinks about it." Maybe you have said that yourself. If you have, I am sure you ended up in the same place I did. I made friends angry. I hurt girlfriends. I stormed off and lived my life my way. Do you know what happened?

At 25 years of age, I found myself all alone. I was broke, busted and disgusted! I had no one to call a friend. I had no one to turn to when the chips were down. I had no one to help me when I fell. Do you know why? Because for eight long years, I lived a selfish lifestyle. I was all about me. I was more concerned about what I wanted and how I felt and how I thought than anyone else around me. I didn't care if I hurt my girlfriends. I didn't care if I made my friends angry. I didn't care about anyone or anything as much as I cared about me.

Selfish! Selfish! Selfish!

An old Chinese saying goes: "The man who is all wrapped up in himself makes a very small package."

That's true! The smallest, least significant people you will ever meet are the ones who can't stop thinking and talking about themselves. Their plans, their adventures, their lives and their thoughts comprise all they know. Don't you find that boring? Isn't that a turn-off? I mean, really: if I wanted to hear your life story, I would have asked you for it!

That's the self-life. Self is all about me, me, me! We're selfish people. We may not mean to be.

But we get that way real quick, don't we? Our fleshly character yearns for attention. And we indulge ourselves more often than not.

   Listen to the thief on the cross next to Jesus. He said: "We're getting what we deserve!"
   He knew he was a thief. He had been caught, tried and convicted. His sentence was to die by crucifixion. He wasn't making excuses. He didn't try to lie his way out of trouble. There was nowhere to run, nowhere to go. He was at the end of his road here on Earth and he knew it. So he confessed and admitted he was being punished for what he had done. He was the last honest thief you'll ever read about.
   Here was a man who lived selfishly. He took from others what he wanted. Now he was paying the ultimate price for his crime. He who TOOK so selfishly from others was now having his life TAKEN from him. In his final hour, at the end of a life filled with selfishness and greed, he has this amazing moment of moral clarity. He confesses that he is suffering justly. Plus, he realizes the only hope of his salvation in the next world is to cry out for mercy. But he does not cry out to the Roman soldiers standing there. Nor does he cry out to the Jews watching him suffer. No, he turns to the man at his side, the lonely carpenter from Galilee. He turns to Jesus, and he asks to be remembered in Paradise.
   This is a picture of a man who is repenting of his sins. This is a man who has run out of options. In the last hour of his life, he has turned to

the Lord. He who TOOK from so many others all his life now asks to be GIVEN something he knows he doesn't deserve.

We are all in need of repentance. The Bible teaches us that in Hebrew (which is the language the Old Testament was written in) the word for "repent" means:
to change the direction you are traveling, to go the opposite direction.
In Greek (the language the New Testament was written in) it means:
to change one's mind.
So to repent means: *to change your mind about the way you're living, and turn and go the opposite direction.*
Some people think it means to feel bad about what you have done. Or to say you are sorry for something you've said. But that is not repentance. That's guilt and an apology.

Repentance means change, a change of heart that leads to a change in your lifestyle.

Listen to the rebuke in verse 40.

But the other criminal rebuked him. "Don't you fear God," he said, "since you are under the same sentence?"

That man rebuked his fellow thief for taunting Jesus.
"You're under the same sentence!" he says.

In other words, the sentence of death. Both men were condemned to die. He tells his partner, "Don't make fun of this man. Don't you fear God?"

Now that's an interesting question to ask. "Don't you fear God?"

Why do you think he asked that question? Did he know something the other man didn't know? Could he see something the other man couldn't see? Did he sense something in his spirit about Christ that was different from other men he'd met?

You see the confession in verse 41.

"We are punished justly, for we are getting what our deeds deserve."

Boy, isn't that refreshing? It's amazing how many people do things wrong and never admit their guilt. They never own up to anything. They'll say things that are terrible. They'll do things that are horrible. But ask if they did it, and they'll shrug their shoulders, and act like they don't know what you're talking about.

Not here! Here is an honest thief. Here is a man acknowledging he is guilty, and justly deserving the punishment he's getting.

Listen to his acknowledgement in verse 41.

"But this man has done nothing wrong."

Isn't that amazing? Here is a guy who is sinful, a guy who *knows* he has done wrong. He is going to die for his sins. Still, even in the midst of suffering, in the trauma of being bled to death, he acknowledges Jesus is sinless. He knows there is something different about the Nazarene. His spirit is in sync with Christ's Holy Spirit.

And that's the way it is with us and the people of this world. They don't have to be around you too long to realize there is something different about you. They don't have to hear you preach or hear you pray to know you've got a different spirit in you. There's something special about you, something unique. That's God's Holy Spirit. He indwells you just as He indwelt Jesus. He made a difference that day on the cross. And He makes a difference for us, too. Hallelujah!

Next, he makes a request in verse 42.

"Remember me when You come into Your Kingdom."

Wow, what a statement! What a request! I call that the Magnificent Request. In all the Bible, that's a bonafide show-stopper.

"Remember me when You come into Your Kingdom."

Remember me – that's the first part. Isn't that a great thing to say to the Lord?

"Lord, remember me."

It makes me feel good to know that I am on His mind. How about you?

"Remember me when You come into Your Kingdom."

He is saying, "Lord, I want You thinking about me when You walk into Your Kingdom. When You step into glory, I want to be on Your mind. Jesus, think of me when You step from this world into the next. When You walk into Your royal palace, I want to be uppermost in Your thoughts." Isn't that a wonderful request?

And now look at the glorious promise Jesus makes in verse 43. There on the cross, with that wood against his back, with nails piercing his flesh, covered in sweat and bleeding from His wounds, filled with pain and agony, Jesus looks into this young thief's eyes and promises:

"This day you shall be with Me in Paradise."

Man, what a promise!
What a guarantee!
What a hope!
Jesus the Christ, the Son of God, the Creator of the universe, the eternal Word from everlasting to everlasting stops all time and proclaims: "This day – not tomorrow, not someday, no, *this* day, you will be with Me . . ."

Not ". . . might be with Me".
Not " . . . I hope you will be with Me".
Not " . . . maybe you can be with Me."
No, He says: "You *will* be with Me in Paradise."

Hallelujah! Praise God!
What finality! What a resolution!

Is there any doubt where that man's soul went when he breathed his last on this earth?

Fortunately, that man's fate can be ours as well. Paradise wasn't made just for him. No, beloved: the Lord made Paradise for all of us to come and live with Him. He longs for our company. He seeks our fellowship.

Heaven is a home for His children to enjoy His presence.

Imagine being in Paradise with God.

Imagine a street of gold and the crystal sea.

Imagine His majestic throne and the power that radiates out from Him and permeates everything around Him.

Not just that. There are loved ones you've missed who have gone before you. They will be there but they will be healthy and well. They'll be happy and not sad. They don't suffer anymore. They'll be joyful and so glad to see you.

There will be saints there who stood strong for the Lord, who faithfully served and gave, and were supernaturally blessed by God down through the church's history. You will meet and get to know them! And their stories -- their testimonies of God's unfailing grace -- will inspire and encourage you. They'll cause you to sing louder and longer the high praises of God than you have ever sung before.

However the greatest moment of all – the best minute of your life ever -- will be when you look upon the King of Kings and Lord of Lords.

When you see the holy Lamb of God, the

Great Shepherd who will turn to you and smile. When you look into the eyes of the One who saw eternity and your place in it and moved toward you, you'll know what Heaven is all about. When you touch His hand and feel the dynamic power flowing out of Him and into you, you'll shout! When deep waves of abiding love sweep over you so strongly you're hardly able to stand, you'll know you're in Paradise.

Yes, when that light that is so bright that it lights up all of Heaven hits you, and you glow in eternal grace, then you'll know Who you're standing next to.

When He wraps His arms around you, and hugs you, you'll smell the frankincense and myrrh in his robe. You'll hear Him say: "I've waited so long for this moment." Yes, that will be the greatest moment.

The thief experienced this because he repented of his sins and acknowledged who Jesus was. And, in like manner, when we repent of our sins and clear our hearts before God, then we too can enter into this intimate relationship with the Father and walk in glory before Him.

We will see some very interesting people when we get to Heaven. However, when we see that thief -- the one that hung on his own cross next to our Lord's on that dark day -- his face . . . will look . . . like ours!

For you see, we are all thieves. We've all, in one way or another, taken advantage of God's goodness and kindness toward us and said, and done and thought things we shouldn't have. We've all taken credit for things He's done. We've all failed to give God glory for what He has blessed us with. We deserve death. Paul says in Romans 6:23:

For the wages of sin is death.

We're all sinners. We're all thieves. Selfish ones, at that. We don't rob from the rich to give to the poor like Robin Hood. No, we heap it on ourselves, don't we? We deserve death every bit as much as that thief did that died next to Christ.

But just as the Lord made a way for that thief to be saved and to escape Hell, so He has made a way for us also. When we confess our sins, and acknowledge His lordship over our lives, when we cry out for mercy, then we're promised His gracious salvation.

Like the thief on the cross, our lives can be marvelous examples of God's grace.

Chapter 2: When I See the Blood, I Will Pass Over You

Exodus 12: 5-7, 12-13

"The animals you choose must be year-old males without defect, and you may take them from the sheep or the goats. Take care of them until the fourteenth day of the month, when all the people of the community of Israel must slaughter them at twilight. Then they are to take some of the blood and put it on the sides and tops of the doorframes of the houses where they eat the lambs . . .

"On that same night I will pass through Egypt and strike down every firstborn—both men and animals—and I will bring judgment on all the gods of Egypt. I am the LORD. **The blood will be a sign for you on the houses where you are; and when I see the blood, I will pass over you.** *No destructive plague will touch you when I strike Egypt."*

In our world there are two forces at war with each other. The Kingdom of God has attacked and is fighting against the Kingdom of Darkness. God's army is advancing His Kingdom throughout the world by the Church. Satan's influence in the world resists our righteous outreach. If you have been born again as a child of God, you were born on a battlefield. You were born in a state of war. The Lord has rescued you from the Devil. But the Devil has not forgotten about you. Nor will he give up trying to get you back. From this point forward, you are caught in the crossfire of two majestic forces – God on the one side, the devil on the other.

This battle didn't begin with us, however. Way back in Exodus, we can read where the devil fought against the Lord. God through Moses wanted to get His people out of Egypt. Satan through Pharaoh resisted his efforts. This was not a personality conflict between two stubborn men. This was a cosmic battle taking place in the spirit realm manifesting itself on the ground in ancient Egypt.

The Egyptians worshipped a variety of gods. One by one, through the various plagues He sent against the Egyptians, God was unseating them in the eyes of their worshipers, and proving His sovereign power. Nine plagues struck them. They dealt with blood in their water, frogs, sores on themselves and their animals as well as locusts. But now they came to the final judgment. God would send His Angel of Death to sweep over the land. He warned the Jewish people through Moses that the firstborn of the livestock and the children would be struck dead by morning.

This was God's final judgment on the Egyptians and their false gods. It all could have been avoided had Pharaoh relented and let the slaves go and worship in the wilderness. But he would not. So the Lord sent the final and most devastating blow. He instructed His people through Moses to kill a lamb or a goat and spread its blood over the doorposts of their homes. He made them this promise: "When I see the blood, I will pass over you."

On this night, the Lord sends His Angel of Death down to take the lives of all of the firstborn. The Jewish people living in the land of Goshen (a province of Egypt) smear the blood of their sacrifice over their doorposts.

Moses promises the people:

"When the LORD goes through the land to strike down the Egyptians, He will see the blood on the top and sides of the doorframe, and will pass over that doorway, and He will not permit the Destroyer to enter your houses and strike you down."
(Exodus 12: 23)

That evening the Word of the Lord came to pass. In Exodus 12: 29-30, we read:

At midnight the LORD struck down all the firstborn in Egypt, from the firstborn of Pharaoh, who sat on the throne, to the firstborn of the prisoner, who was in the dungeon, and the firstborn of all the livestock as well. Pharaoh and all his officials and all the Egyptians got up during the night, and there was loud wailing in Egypt, for there was not a house without someone dead.

This was a terrible night. Even though the Egyptians were idolaters in that they worshiped foreign gods that were not really gods at all but demons posing as gods, it is still sad and tragic that so many of them lost their firstborn children needlessly. I can imagine the crying and screaming when the dead bodies were found. Even Pharaoh himself was not spared. He woke in the night to discover his own son, who was in the line of succession to become the next pharaoh was dead. So many tears were shed that night. So many groans flowed from broken hearts that evening. Lives and families were changed forever. If you have ever known anyone who has lost a child you know many of those Egyptians probably wished it had been themselves who had died and not their children.

Blood is a precious thing. Without it, you cannot live. Blood carries everything through your circulatory system that you need to survive and thrive. If you lose blood, you begin losing vital energy, oxygen and nutrients you need to be healthy. If you continue to bleed, it will not be long before you die. So blood is precious. God designed us to need it.

All through the Old Testament when He was dealing with the Israelites, He kept reiterating to them how important it was that their sins be rolled back on a yearly basis through the shedding of blood. The priests sacrificed bulls, goats, sheep and birds. All of it was for the remission of sin. The Bible tells us:

Without the shedding of blood, there is no remission for sin. (Hebrews 9:22)

In other words, there was no forgiveness if some sort of sacrifice was not made on their behalf.

What the Lord was doing in the Old Testament was pointing toward something new He would institute in the New Testament. The blood of the animals was a "type" or foreshadowing of something He had in mind for a New Covenant He would reveal through Christ. And that was how the blood of Jesus, poured out on your behalf on Mount Calvary would wash away not only your sins but all the sins of mankind forever!

Jesus was the Lord's perfect lamb, a man with a human nature but who never sinned. (Hebrews 4:15) When He died on that wooden cross, He died for you and me. He died for all the sins we've committed, all the sins we're committing and all the sins we'll commit in the future.

His blood perfectly cleanses us from the stain of sin. Through it we are justified before God. (Romans 5:9) *Justified* means: "just-as-if-I'd" never sinned before God. When we repent of our sins and ask the Lord for forgiveness, He so thoroughly scrubs us clean with the blood of Jesus that He can no longer see the sin or the stain it made. That does not mean all the consequences of your actions go away too. It means that God the Father chooses not to remember our sins any longer. He casts them into a sea of forgetfulness, nevermore mentioned in Heaven. (Micah 7:19)

It is important for us to realize the great extent to which the blood of Jesus cleans us. It isn't just a simple washing. It is a thorough purging of the sin and the stain that goes with it. It is entirely erased from the mind of God. Therefore, it should be removed from our thinking as well. It makes no sense for us to punish ourselves for something the Lord has forgiven and forgotten. If our Father chooses not to think about it any longer, why should we?

I hope you see how wonderful the cleansing and how necessary the washing is of our souls by the blood of Jesus. It was precious in God's sight. (I Peter 1:19) It was the blood of His son. It was not something surrendered easily or quickly but it was lavished on you and me. It is so powerful, that it has enough strength to go on forgiving us and forgiving everyone who ever sins against us for as long as we live.

How? Because it is supernaturally empowered by the Holy Ghost.

When we get saved and are born into God's family, we are washed in the blood of Jesus just as surely as a newborn baby fresh from its mother's womb is covered in her blood. His supernatural blood automatically washes away all of our sins. And every time afterwards, when we realize we have said something or done something or even thought something that is not pleasing to the Father, we can repent of that sin and ask for forgiveness and the Lord will immediately apply the blood to our souls. We are cleansed through and through. (I John 1:9)

Discover the power of Jesus' blood working in your life by examining how the blood affected the Jewish people in ancient Egypt that fateful night.

His Blood Covering Provides Protection

> *"On that same night I will pass through Egypt and strike down every firstborn—both men and animals—and I will bring judgment on all the gods of Egypt. I am the LORD. The blood will be a sign for you on the houses where you are; and when I see the blood, I will pass over you. No destructive plague will touch you when I strike Egypt."*
> (Exodus 12:12-13)

Just as the blood of lambs and goats protected the people from evil that evening so Jesus' blood protects us from evil as well. When we plead the blood of Jesus, a supernatural shield of protection surrounds us. Satan and his demonic forces can attack in a variety of ways. But you are safe and secure from harm by the invisible shield of armor that is the blood of Christ.

I urge you to plead the blood of Jesus over you and your loved ones every day when you first get out of bed. Don't walk around being vulnerable. Plead his blood over your mind, your heart and your eyes so a helmet of divine grace will protect your eyes and your thoughts from the devil's onslaught.

The blood of the lambs and goats protected the Israelites from the Angel of Death that night. The first born of the Egyptians died because they were not under the blood. The Angel of Death had a clear shot at them and he took it! There was no protection or shield. They had no barrier or wall to guard them from impending death. However, in Jesus' blood, the saints of God have that protective wall. We are shielded and hidden from the devil. He wants to kill us. But Jesus offers abundant life. (John 10:10)

How can we protect ourselves and our loved ones from the death-dealer? Be covered in the precious blood of Jesus. It is the only substance the enemy cannot penetrate.

His Blood Covering Gives Us Freedom

When any human being is born, they are born into sin. What that means is we all have a sin nature. As we grow older, various temptations come our way. The lust of the flesh, the lust of the eyes and the pride of life trip us up and tempt us to sin. It is inevitable. We can't stop it. We are weak in our flesh and will be until the day we die and leave this world forever. That is why ministers refer to us as being "bound by sin". What they mean is: we are chained to our desires that lure us to habitual sinning. We are caught. We are stuck. We can't get loose from it on our own. It is impossible.

This is what Paul meant when he wrote:

What shall we conclude then? Are we any better? Not at all! We have already made the charge that Jews and Gentiles alike are all under sin.
(Romans 3:9)

All of us are under sin. We've all failed God. None of us are sinless. It is almost as if in the spirit world, when you are born, you are born in prison, chained to a wall, and there is no hope of escape.

I saw a television program of a group of women who were arrested in Columbia for trafficking in narcotics. They tried to smuggle drugs out of the country and were arrested, tried, convicted and sentenced to prison. So here they were in this little women's prison in Columbia. They were from all over the world. There were American women there, Germans, Swedes, Central and South American women, too.

I noticed there were children running around in the background. As I watched, I wondered: what kind of prison is this? I've never heard of a prison with kids in it.

As I continued to watch, the narrator explained that in Columbia, if you are a woman with kids -- and you go to prison -- unless there is someone in your family or in your community who is willing (and financially able) to take them in and care for them, when you get sent to prison, the kids go with you! The children remain there with their mother until someone offers to take them and raise them. If no one offers to help, the kids stay in prison and serve time with their mother!

Can you believe it? I was shocked when I saw this. Later on in the show, they showed an American nun who felt called to reach out to the prison kids. She got permission from the warden to set up a classroom. The kids were brought in every day, and she taught them how to read, write, count and spell. She taught them about nature, science, nutrition, and even ethical behavior like knowing the difference between right and wrong, treating others the way they wanted to be treated. They allowed her to teach from the Bible as well. They showed the kids singing Christian songs, learning scriptures and doing their regular school work.

    It was truly amazing, an eye-opening experience for me. The reason I mention it is because of those children. As I watched that program, the one thing that struck me was: *they have no idea what real life is like!* If you were born or raised in prison from a very early age, you would have no concept of what life is like on the outside. You would think being in jail was normal. You would think everyone is surrounded by a tall fence and guarded by men and women with guns everyday. Those kids had no idea they were in a prison. Since they had never been out of a prison, they didn't know they were locked up in one.

    Can you imagine what they would have said if you had told them: "In other places, you can leave and walk all day, and no one will stop you or make you go back?" They would probably look at you like you were crazy. Imagine what they would think if you said, "Most people don't have iron bars where they live."

    When we are born into this world, we are born as slaves to sin. We are trapped by our desires, and bound by the devil in an invisible prison. Unfortunately, we don't know we're prisoners because we're born in here. This is all we've ever known. We weren't born free and trapped later. No, we were born in sin. We were born in trouble.

Unless someone rescues us, we will live and die in sin in a devil's Hell for eternity.

But the blood of Jesus is the power that sets us free from bondage! The power that is in His blood breaks the chains that bind us and frees us to love and worship Him as were meant to do. His blood delivers us from evil. His blood sets us free from the iron grip of sin. His blood releases us to become the men and women He has destined for us to be in His Kingdom.

We are free from bondage to sin. If it is alcohol, we are freed from it. Hallelujah! If it is drugs, we've been released from them. Thank God! If it is pornography, we have been delivered from it.

Overeating? Spending compulsively?
Cursing? Lying?
Cheating? Stealing?
Running from responsibility?

Whatever your sin is, there is power in the blood of Jesus to break the yoke of bondage off of your life and set you free to love, serve, give and minister to others. Thank God for the precious blood of Jesus! It is the key that unlocks the prison doors. It is the gate swung wide open. It is our escape route, our exit out of sin and darkness and entrance into righteousness and His marvelous light!

His Blood Cleanses the Deepest Sin

But if we walk in the light, as he is in the light, we have fellowship with one another, and the blood of Jesus, his Son, purifies us from all sin. (I John 1:7)

The supernatural power in Jesus' blood also cleanses us or purifies us from all sin. Whatever your sin may be, it has been washed from you for good. God the Father chooses not to dwell on it any longer. You are thoroughly purged from the inside out. If you could look at the book in Heaven that records your sins, the pages would be blank on all the ones you've asked forgiveness for. The Lord said:

"No more shall every man teach his neighbor, and every man his brother, saying, 'Know the Lord,' for they all shall know Me, from the least of them to the greatest of them, says the Lord. For I will forgive their iniquity, and their sin I WILL REMEMBER THEIR NO MORE." (Jeremiah 31:34)

And He meant it!
Not only does the blood of Christ remove sin, it also cleans away the guilt associated with it. Many people have asked for forgiveness from the Lord and received it. He is merciful. But they do not believe they are forgiven.
Sometimes this is because they have not forgiven themselves. But if you have truly repented from sin, and asked the Lord to forgive you, you can rest assured He has done so. (I John 1:9)

The Lord does not hold grudges. As bad as you believe your sin may be, His Word says He will forgive when you seek forgiveness from Him. It is egotistical to think that you can sin so badly that God cannot forgive you.

God is bigger than you are. His righteousness and mercy are larger than your sin and wickedness. There is nothing you can do that someone hasn't already done. There is no thought you can think, no word you can speak or action you can take that hasn't already been done before. So God is not shocked or surprised at your sinfulness. He is never taken aback at your failure. That is not to say that He will turn a blind eye or a deaf ear to your sin. Nor shall He ever approve of it or forgive you because you're human. No, He forgives His children when they lower themselves and come to Him and ask for forgiveness. When they truly repent and seek His grace and favor again, then He forgives -- and He forgets.

Some people don't believe they are forgiven because they have sinned against someone else and that person has not forgiven them.

Carolyn didn't believe that the Lord could forgive her. She had done something in her youth to hurt her mother severely. She slept with her boyfriend and became pregnant. Instead of owning up to her failure and admitting it, she fled and tried to hide her sin. She told her mother she was going to move in with an aunt in another town to go to school. In reality, she was moving there to have her baby and keep her pregnancy hidden.

Eventually, her mother found out. When she did, she was devastated. She had raised her daughter in church and to have conservative, moral values. She was not only shocked that her daughter had engaged in premarital sex but that she was pregnant with a man's child with whom she was no longer in contact.

Carolyn's mother wrote her a long letter expressing her embarrassment and dissatisfaction. She reminded her of their social standing in the community, and how that was now ruined because of her selfish actions. She never quite said she didn't forgive or couldn't. But Carolyn was left with the feeling that she would not be forgiven nor would she or the child ever be welcome in the home.

Carolyn had her baby. With the help of her aunt, she moved away to the other side of the country, and made a life for herself and her child. In time she married and had other children, and raised them as well. In all those years, she longed to speak with her mother, and see her again but she never did. She was afraid to call for fear of rejection. She sent cards on her mother's birthday and at Christmas but never received any back. She also sent brief letters with pictures when the children had their birthdays. Her mother never responded.

Although it was very hard for her to do so, she eventually gave up on the idea of ever having a relationship with her mother. She found other older women with whom she bonded and who became pseudo-grandmothers to her children.

Eventually her mother passed away, and after returning from the funeral, Carolyn felt as if now she would never be forgiven for her past sin.

Two things to note about Carolyn's story.

(1) After asking God for forgiveness for her sexual immorality, Carolyn was forgiven. The Bible teaches that once you ask for forgiveness from the Lord, He forgives you. So at that point, she was clean. She still felt the burden of her sin because she had not forgiven herself. Plus, her pregnancy was evidence of her sin. Also, she didn't apologize or ask her mother's forgiveness. Apparently, that was harder than speaking to God about her problem. Maybe she knew her mother would judge her instead of forgiving her. God forgave Carolyn, and was anxious to restore the broken fellowship He'd enjoyed with her in the past.

(2) Carolyn made the mistake of assuming her mother was God in her life. Not consciously but subconsciously, she placed her mother on the throne of her heart, and acknowledged that if her mother did not forgive her, she would not (could not) be forgiven. Knowing her mother was not a person who easily forgave (unlike the Lord she served), instead of repenting to her mother and clearing the air with her, she chose instead to run away and not confront the issue.

It is our responsibility to repent and ask for forgiveness. Not only from the Lord, but also from

anyone we may hurt. People we sin with need to hear it, too. Once we realize we're wrong,
> admit we're sorry,
> ask for forgiveness
> and offer to make restitution,

we've done all the Lord requires us to do. It is not our responsibility to make someone forgive us. Nor is it our responsibility to explain things until they make sense. Or to lie and throw the blame for what we've done in someone else's lap. The Lord expects us to admit what we've done and seek forgiveness. If the other person (or people) we're repenting to choose(s) not to forgive or forget, that is between them and the Lord. We can't make them forgive us. Nor can we make them forget. We can ask for mercy but whether they grant it or not is up to them.

Had Carolyn realized her mother was not God, it may have been easier for her to say, "I am sorry I disappointed you. I disappointed myself. But I can't go back and change the past. I have a future with this child, and I'll live in that future with the baby. If you can forgive me that is wonderful. If not, that's okay. I will go on and so will you. But I will have lost a mother, and you will have lost a daughter and a grandchild.

"I ask you to forgive me, and love me and the baby. If you can't, the Lord will provide someone who can."

If you are struggling with the feeling of being unforgiven, is it because you have not asked the Lord for forgiveness? If you have bowed before Him and sought His mercy, He has forgiven you.

He is a God of His Word. He is Who He says He is and He can do what He says He can do.

Are you struggling with feeling unforgiven because someone has not forgiven you? If you are waiting for mercy from someone else, you may be waiting for the rest of your life. No one is under obligation to extend mercy to you except God's children. Some of them fail to do so. The hurt may be too deep. The shock may be too fresh. The wound may be too hard. Maybe later, after some time, they will be able to do so. You're not in control of that. That is between them and the Lord. Once you have apologized and offered to make restitution, all you can do is walk away and leave it in the hands of the Lord to work out.

Maybe you're feeling like you have not been forgiven because you have not forgiven yourself. The devil loves to replay the old tapes of our sins and failures as often as we are willing to listen to them. Understanding you were wrong is the first step toward asking for forgiveness. Dwelling on the greatness of your sin, and feeling overwhelmed by it is not healthy.

You must forgive yourself.

One thing that helps me is to realize that my sin is no greater than any other sin anyone else has committed. My sin is not so spectacular that even God Himself is amazed and bewildered. That plays to your ego if you think you have finally done something even God cannot forgive. The Bible says He is willing to cleanse me when I repent and seek forgiveness. Therefore, I follow the pattern:

1. I admit I am wrong.
2. I say I am sorry (to Him and everyone else I may have hurt).
3. I ask for forgiveness.
4. I offer to make restitution.

After that, according to His Word, I have done all I am supposed to do. Then He does the rest. It is amazingly simple. You may find it hard to forgive yourself but you need to get over it. You're not perfect. You make mistakes every day. This is one more. It may be big. Okay. We acknowledge that. Now, do what His word commands, and get clear of it. God did not put you here to drag around the heavy chains of your past sins for the rest of your life. That is bondage from the enemy. That cripples your service to the King.

If the blood of Jesus cannot clean you from guilt, then it has no power to clean you from sin either. That means Jesus died in vain for all of us, and we are all bound for Hell. That sounds like something Satan would say. But Jesus says he is a liar and the father of lies. (John 8:44) The Bible says Jesus' blood washes away sin AND guilt.

So, is your faith in God's Word . . . or in the devil's lies?

What's Covering You Right Now?

"Whoever believes in the Son has eternal life, but whoever rejects the Son will not see life, for God's wrath remains on him." (John 3:36)

All of us are being covered in the spirit realm by something. According to the Bible, either Jesus' blood is covering you (in which case, you are forgiven and clean) or God's wrath remains on you. So you are either clean or still dirty, covered by your sin in the eyes of God.

You are either free or bound.

You are either under the blood of Christ or facing God's wrath.

The Israelites who obeyed Moses' command to put the blood on their doorposts were covered by the blood. When death and destruction came that night, they were safe. The Egyptians were not covered by the blood. The wrath of God came down on them in the form of the Angel of Death who took the lives of their firstborn. They were under God's judgment.

So what covers you right now? The blood of Jesus? Or the wrath of God?

It is clear that Jesus' blood will wash away your sins. Once applied to your life, you can stand before the Lord in cleanness, wholeness and purity. But until you do, the wrath (or judgment) of God abides (or lives) on you. Until you apply His precious blood, your sin remains, and you are dirty before God.

It is clear that Jesus' blood removes your guilt. Once applied, you stand before your Creator with a clean heart and a renewed spirit. You don't run *from* God. You run *to* Him. Your sleep is peaceful because your conscience is clean. But until you do, you will continue to suffer irrational fears and anxieties, and even have nightmares. Until you apply His precious blood, all sorts of mental, emotional, psychological and physical maladies will torment you because you stand guilty before a righteous Judge.

It is clear the blood of Jesus protects us from death and destruction. Once applied to our lives, a wall or shield is erected between us and the destroyer. No one can harm us unless the Father permits it. He will not allow anything to come upon us that we cannot handle by His grace. Until the blood is applied, it is open season for the devil and his demon spirits to torment, torture and murder you. You have no protection, no safeguard against his schemes.

Applying the Blood

Fortunately, applying the blood of Christ to your life isn't some great secret or a scientific formula. There are two things we must do:

1. **Appropriate the blood of Jesus by faith.**

Jesus' blood is a force and power we grasp hold of by asking for it. The Father is generous and withholds nothing sacred from His children. Confess to the Lord right now this simple declaration:

"Father, I come before your throne under the shed blood of your Son, Jesus. And I ask you to cover me with His atoning blood.

"I need it not only to wash away my sins but also to surround me and protect me from all harm. I need the power in Your blood to deliver me from evil and empower me to stand for you.

"Your Word says when I pray, I must believe that I am receiving it even as I speak it. Right now, I step out in faith and declare the power in the blood of Jesus is resident in my life. I am saved, forgiven, delivered, healed and able to do all things through Christ who strengthens me. I thank you, in Jesus' Name. Amen."

If you prayed that prayer with sincerity, the Lord has already heard and answered you. At this moment, the power that lives in Christ's blood lives in you!

2. Apply it to you and yours.

Put the blood over everyone in your family and all you own. Put it over your church and your city. Don't be afraid you'll use it up. The Lord has plenty of power. Put the blood over your work station, your class room, your office building, and your place of business.

John Osteen, the former pastor of Lakewood Church in Houston, Texas said one day his wife, Dodie told him one of the children was sick. He got angry. Not at the child or his wife. He got mad at the devil.

He said: "It seemed like every time the Lord opened a door for me to go somewhere and preach, the devil attacked someone in my family with illness."

Bro. Osteen went on to say he got good and mad at the devil. How dare he attack his children!

"So, I lined all the kids up behind me and we walked all over our property, every square inch of that house. And then outside the house. We looked like a choo-choo train with a bunch of little cars. There was me and Dodie, and then each of the children from the oldest down to the youngest. I'm sure the neighbors thought we were crazy!

"But I set my foot down and every time I did, I said: 'I put the blood, I put the blood, I put the blood.'"

Brother Osteen was convinced that there was still power in the blood to heal his family and make the devil get off his property.

Guess what happened?

That season of sickness was broken off his family! That is not to say that none of them ever got sick again. But the constant repetition of the children getting ill and having to go to the doctor ceased. Then Brother Osteen was able to travel and minister without worrying over his children any longer.

I encourage you to put your foot down in your home, in your car, in your family, in your finances and in your health. Don't let the devil steal what God has given you. Put your foot down in your marriage and in all of your relationships. And when you do, say:

"I put the blood, I put the blood, I put the blood . . ."

Put the blood of Jesus on everything and everyone that is in your life. God will sanctify it and bless it. If it is someone living in sin, the convicting power of the Holy Ghost will convince them of their sinfulness and the guilt in their heart will increase. Put the blood over your heart, your mind, soul and spirit. Plead the blood over your pastor and your church. Plead it over your children and extended family.

There is no power on Earth that can withstand and resist the power that is in the blood of Jesus. He is God's perfect lamb offered as a sacrifice for you and me. When God sees the blood of His Son on our homes and over our hearts, He will make the devil pass over us.

"A thousand may fall at my side, and ten-thousand at my right hand, but it shall not come near me."
(Psalm 91:7)

Chapter 3: In the Shadow of the Cross

In the Shadow

When I was in sixth grade I had a teacher named Mr. Moore. Mr. Moore had taught my older brother, David the year before. My brother David was what we in Texas refer to as a "pistol". By that I mean, he was a little trouble-maker. The first to get in a fist fight. The first to cut class or skip school altogether. The first to speak out if he disagreed with you. David was a real pistol, and all the sixth grade teachers remembered him. Quite naturally, when I came along, they saw the family resemblance. They saw the last name. Similar height. Similar build.

What do you think they were thinking?

From the first day of school, I got these looks from my teachers. Looks of doubt. Looks of suspicion. They would immediately rearrange their classrooms. I was pulled out of the alphabetical order we usually sat in, and made to sit as near the teacher's desk as possible. Why? Because they figured that since David was my brother, I would act like him and they were ready to pounce on any trouble I might start for the new school year.

The truth was that I was very different from my older brother. Once you got to know us, you would have seen that we were about as different as two brothers could be. The way we dressed, the music we listened to, our hobbies and our choice of friends could not have been more different. The teachers were all expecting us to be two peas in a pod. In actuality, I was a whole lot different than my brother. I had a lot of favor with my teachers. I didn't realize it at the time but I did. I would like to think it was my charm and wit than won them over. The truth was I kept my mouth shut, paid attention, got along with the other kids and tried my best in school. As a result, they thought I was an angel. (My wife and kids would argue that with you!)

I mention this because I grew up in the shadow of my older brother. I could not escape his reputation. I want to share with you a message called "In the Shadow of the Cross". And I want you to see how all of us now live in the shadow of Christ's cross.

We're marked by it. It influences what we say and do. It registers and identifies us in the eyes of the world for the rest of our lives. We're powerless to prevent that.

On Mount Calvary

The Bible tells us it took place on a windswept hill just outside of Jerusalem over two-thousand years ago. The crowds jeered and mocked as Jesus carried his cross up the hill. We're not sure what sort of day it was. When I picture the scene, I hear dry wind blowing over those barren hills in Judea. I see a clear sky -- though we do not know what the sky looked like. It may have been overcast. The writers of the Gospel accounts don't give us a weather report.

We know the members of the Sanhedrin were there. The Pharisees and Sadducees were successful in getting Jesus condemned to death. I am not sure if Annas and Caiaphas were in the crowd that went to the top of the hill to see the bloody spectacle. The accounts are silent as to their whereabouts during those final hours of Jesus' mortal life. They may have been there or they may have decided that their work was done. They may have chosen to remain in the background and observe from afar.

The Roman guards in charge of executions were there. They would have pushed and prodded the condemned to hurry up and walk faster so they could get to the top of the hill and finish them off. The sooner they got them nailed to the crosses, the sooner they would die and the guards could go home.

Members of Jesus' family were there as well as some of his disciples.

Imagine the tiredness He must have felt, having been up all night, and the pain that coursed through His body from the beating and whipping He had taken. Scripture relates how He carried the beam upon His shoulders as far as He could. When His human strength failed him, the soldiers forced a man from Cyrene named Simon to carry it the rest of the way. No doubt Jesus was delirious, on the brink of total physical collapse.

The punches He had taken to the face as the guards laughed and asked: "Prophesy, who hit you then?" had marred His features. One

Messianic prophecy refers to His beard having been pulled out. (Isa. 50:6) The crown of thorns that rested on His brow cut His skin and made it bleed. It probably created an unending headache that throbbed relentlessly until He died. Can you imagine His busted lips, swollen and bruised? Perhaps His teeth were chipped from the punches He endured. His nose may have been broken by then, which would have bled and made breathing difficult. His eyes were probably blackened and swollen shut like a boxer at the end of a losing prizefight.

You may have endured the tying of your hands to the beam. How about when they drove the iron nails through your wrists, bursting arteries and veins as they secured you to that rough wood? Could you have stayed conscious when they slammed the base of the post into the hole in the ground?

Jesus hung there, suspended between Earth and Heaven for six long hours that day, from 9:00 a.m. until 3:00 p.m. Birds circled overhead. The crowd laughed, taunting and heckling Him. Some wept and left. Others stayed and watched. The wind blew. Time passed. The thieves mocked and pled. The soldiers drank and gambled.

It has been said that the hardest thing to do is wait for something. If that's true, that must have been the longest six hours of Jesus' life; hanging there, waiting –

    not for rescue
    not for comfort

no . . .
He was waiting to die.

Pain

In the shadow of the cross there is pain, both physical and emotional. If we are going to serve God with our whole hearts and submit our lives to Him, we are going to suffer. And sometimes, it will feel like you're dying.

Later, knowing that all was now completed, and so that the Scripture would be fulfilled, Jesus said, "I am thirsty." A jar of wine vinegar was there, so they soaked a sponge in it, put the sponge on a stalk of the hyssop plant, and lifted it to Jesus' lips. (John 19:28-29)

They always brought a mixture of wine and vinegar when they crucified the criminals. They stuck a sponge on the end of a rod, and dipped the sponge into the bucket of wine and vinegar, and raised it to the lips of the dying. This was their way of trying to help the condemned men. They wanted the wine to numb the feelings so they would not have to suffer as badly as if they were stone-cold sober.
Jesus knew the end was near. He knew *". . . all was now completed . . ." (v. 28)*

His service to God had led to this. There were nails in His body, through His wrists and feet. A crown of thorns adorned His head, mocking His majesty. He'd been beaten and whipped.

We want to believe that in following God there will be an end to pain and suffering. We like to think that the Lord will cover us and protect us from hurting. Such is simply not the case. There is a death to self that is called for. The Lord demands we come to an end of ourselves in His service. **This Christian walk is a journey wherein you slowly but surely -- through the passing of time – (and the enduring of trials) lose the self-life and take on the Christ- life.** Sometimes you will be publicly praised for what you have done for Him. Sometimes you may receive applause. Other times you will be ignored for what you've accomplished . . . or perhaps even criticized. You may even be subjected to public disapproval and ridicule. Don't think that can't happen to you. If Jesus had to endure it, there is no reason we won't. We aren't better than our Master.

Yes, in the shadow of the cross, there is shame and pain, humiliation and loss. But there is also glory, and the anointing and the tender hand of God to lift you up and strengthen you in your darkest hour. Remember, weeping may endure for an evening, but joy – Joy – JOY comes in the morning!

For His anger is but for a moment, His favor is for life; weeping may endure for a night but joy comes in the morning. (Psalm 30:5)

There is pain in the shadow of the cross.

Provision

Near the cross of Jesus stood his mother, his mother's sister, Mary the wife of Clopas, and Mary Magdalene. When Jesus saw his mother there, and the disciple whom he loved standing nearby, he said to his mother, 'Dear woman, here is your son." (John 19:25-26)

    It amazes me that even in the midst of His greatest pain and suffering, Jesus was thinking of others. As He bleeds and slowly dies, He sees His mother and John. His strength is waning. His vision is weakening. He directs her to cling to John as she would cling to Him. He cares for the widows, orphans, and grieving parents, too. He did not want to leave this world without making sure there was someone to take care of His mother in his absence.
    He is still that way. He will not allow any of us to go without as long as there is someone to care for us. And He will search the world to find someone to care for us.
    Look at the provision He makes for His mother. He makes sure she has a man to care for her. In those days, a woman could not make it on her own. She needed a man to protect and support her. His father, Joseph was probably dead. Now He was dying. So -- in effect -- He arranged for an adoption to take place. Not for a

child. No, for a parent. He wanted His mother to be looked after. He knew John would do so.

He looked upon Mary, and her sister, Mary the wife of Clopas. He looked down upon Mary Magdalene, and John, the disciple whom He loved. He had compassion and mercy for them. He was concerned about their welfare, their future. Even as He hung there, His life ebbing away, He focused on *their* needs and not His own.

Jesus gave Mary, His mother to John to take care for and look after because she needed someone to care for her. We all need someone to care for us. In the shadow of the cross, there is great provision from the Master's hand. Our every need will be supplied when we kneel in its shadow.

There is abundant provision for our needs in the shadow of the cross.

Privilege

Many people shirk away from responsibility, especially ones that tax the soul and the purse. Most of us only care for our children and our parents. Can you imagine the tremendous responsibility that was laid upon John's shoulders that day? You are given the assignment of not only caring for your friends' mother but the mother of the Son of God! She was well known. It wasn't like you could go away and disappear with her. Everywhere you took her, there would inevitably be a follower, a fellow believer who would recognize her or perhaps know her personally. Her welfare was thrust entirely upon him. It was a sacred responsibility, a major, multi-year task.

But what some might consider a burden, others would consider a blessing. What others might withdraw from (those who live the self-life) others receive with pleasure and embrace the task with joy in their hearts. **Because when you live in the shadow of the cross, there is privilege.**

The privilege of serving others.
The privilege of being available to others.
The privilege of sacrificing for others.

If that doesn't sit well with you it may be because you're not serving the Master. You may be serving yourself. As a result, the idea of serving another is repugnant. If you've not bowed to the King, then you won't bow to a fellow servant either. If you won't run an errand for Jesus, you certainly won't do so for a brother or sister in Christ.

Jesus gave John the responsibility and privilege of caring for His mother, Mary. In like manner, He will also give us such assignments. He brings people across our paths who need our help. He expects us to care for them, and see to their needs just as if it were He Himself or His mother that needed assistance. He *burdens* us with these things. But we see them as *privileges*.

As opportunities to bless others.
As opportunities to care for others.

As opportunities to exercise faith and experience His grace.

As a privilege to care for one who needs the Master's love.

It is not a burden or pain to see to other's needs.

It is a privilege to be entrusted with the care of others when you live in the shadow of the cross.

Perception

The centurion, seeing what had happened, praised God and said, "Surely this was a righteous man." (Luke 23:47)

Up until this point in the story, there is no comment from the Roman soldiers. They were there to do a job. There was no halo around Jesus' head to alert them as to who He was. Angels weren't singing at His arrival to let them know they were about to kill the Lord of Life. He looked like any other man in the crowd. Yes, He was beaten and bloody. But they knew how their cohorts treated those condemned to die. Once the judgment was rendered, the life of the condemned was basically worthless. They were free to treat (or mistreat) the criminals any way they chose. It was no surprise and caused no shock to see this one so badly marred.

The Bible tells us this one centurion, when he saw Jesus' last gasp, suddenly perceived who

He really was. Like a bolt of lightening flashing through his mind, he had a moment of cosmic clarity and saw – not just another dying Jew – but the Christ hanging there before him.

Listen to the Gospel writers as they describe it.

Standing in front of Jesus, seeing him breathe out his last breathe, the centurion utters, *"Truly, this man was the son of God!"*
(Matt. 27:54, Mk 15:39)

The centurion, seeing what had happened, praised God and said, *"Surely this was a righteous (or innocent) man." (Luke 23:47)*

In summary, what he said was: "Truly, this man was innocent. He was the son of God!"

Keep in mind, this was not one of Jesus' disciples. This was not a member of His family. This was not a close friend. This man wasn't even a Jew. Up until this day, there is no record he had ever seen or met Jesus before. Now, in the final moment of Jesus' earthly life, on the eve of His return to the spirit world, this lost sinner, a Roman centurion in charge of the crucifixion detail for the day utters: "This man was innocent (or righteous). He was God's son!"

Many people who disagree with Christianity (and some who do not) want to argue and discuss who Jesus was. You can read a lot of books about Him. There are many sermons about Him. There are many opportunities to discuss Him. But you will only see Him clearly when you kneel near the cross.

There is divine perception in the shadow of the cross.

Poverty

Some wonder why Christians focus so much on the cross. After all, it was an instrument of torture and death. Why would you give it so much attention?

You need to understand what the cross represents to understand its significance. For three years, the Lord healed those who were sick. He encouraged those who were downcast. For three years, He blessed those who needed help. He strengthened the weak. He opened blind eyes and deaf ears. He loosened mute tongues, and raised the dead back to life. After Jesus had given out everything He had to give, on this day, His final day, He gave the only thing He had left.

He gave Himself.

He poured out His life and became the divine sacrifice in order that our sins might be forgiven once and for all.

The cross then becomes a symbol, not only of our new birth and freedom in the Kingdom of God but also a place of death.

Death to self and selfishness.

Death to self-centeredness.

Death to a life that revolves only around me, and what I want.

The cross means death to the self-life.

Jesus was put to death on the cross. Earlier He had told his disciples:

"No one takes it from Me, but I lay it down of Myself. I have power to lay it down, and I have power to take it again. This command I have received from My Father." (John 10:18)

Therefore, we can say, Jesus willingly went to the cross and surrendered Himself to death so that we might pass from death to life.

When you come to the end of yourself,

when you get to a place where you no longer believe in your skills and talents,

when you lose faith in you,

when you doubt you can go on,

that's when you realize you're spiritually bankrupt.

You realize you are broke before God.

You have nothing to offer Him He can't get from anyone else. In the presence of God you become aware of just how big He is, and how small you are.

You realize He is the Master, and you are the student.

He is the Father, and you are the child.

He is the leader, and you are the follower.

He is the King!

... And you are a very fortunate slave whose been adopted into the royal family.

But the other criminal rebuked him. "Don't you fear God," he asked, "since you are under the same sentence? We are punished justly, for we are getting what our deeds deserve. But this man has done nothing wrong." Then he said, "Jesus, remember me when you come into your kingdom." Jesus answered him, "I tell you the truth, today you will be with me in paradise." (Luke 23: 40-42)

There were two thieves who were executed on either side of Jesus on that dark day. One of them reviled and mocked him. The other was aware of his spiritual bankruptcy, and his personal wickedness. In his own way, he sought to make things right with God. He tried to find forgiveness. When he asked Jesus to remember him when he entered into His Kingdom, he was acknowledging:

(1) Jesus is a king;
(2) He is the Son of God;
(3) Jesus came from Heaven;
(4) He would return to Heaven;
(5) Jesus could pardon his sin.

In effect, the repentant thief prostrated himself (or lowered himself in his spirit man) and bowed to the Lordship of Christ.

And Jesus seeing this, replied: "This day you will be with Me in Paradise." In other words, Jesus saw his repentance, acknowledged he was forgiven and promised him an eternity in Heaven with Him.

There is poverty of the soul near the cross of Christ.

"Blessed are the poor in spirit, for theirs is the kingdom of Heaven." (Matt. 5:3)

God gives the Kingdom of Heaven to those who are poor in spirit. In the shadow of the cross, you will realize your utter lack – your poverty of spirit.

Promise

Jesus had to go to the cross and die in order to go to Heaven later. In like manner, as we follow our divine example, we have to go the cross and die as well in order to go to Heaven. His cross is symbolic of brokenness and death to self. It is a place where we surrender who we are and what we want to embrace to grasp hold of who He is and what He wants for us.

Jesus promised the penitent thief an entrance into Paradise that day. Listen to Luke describe the scene.

Then he said, "Jesus, remember me when you come into your kingdom". Jesus answered him, "I tell you the truth, today you will be with Me in Paradise." (Luke 23:42-43)

Just as He extended the offer to the thief who repented so He offers the same opportunity to us today. There is no time or space with God. The Bible states He is the same yesterday, today and forever. (Heb. 13:8)

Today, He no longer hangs on a cross. Stephen -- as he was being martyred -- exclaimed he saw the Father sitting on the throne, and one like the Son of Man standing next to it. (Acts 7:55-56) We know Jesus is in Heaven with God but the offer still stands. For anyone who bows their knee in submission and pours out their hearts to Him, He opens the door of Heaven!

He is no respecter of persons. There is no sin you have committed that God cannot forgive. There is nothing you have said or done He is not willing to erase and forget. The Lord is more concerned with the welfare of your soul than what you have done in your past to endanger it.

Just as He was broken, so He is looking for broken people. Just as He was wounded and rejected -- despised by His own people -- so today He is looking for the wounded, the hurt, and the betrayed and angry ones. Those who have been shunned and ignored, those who have been beaten down by the circumstances of life; these are the people Jesus searches for.

Don't try and clean yourself up first. You can't do it. If you could get clean enough to get into Heaven, Jesus would not have had to go to the cross and die. If you come as you are and surrender your life to Him, He will take you, just as you are.

Washing you with the Word, and surrounding you with His love from others, He will cleanse you and make you the person He has designed you to be.

He extends the same invitation to us that He extended to the dying thief next to him that dark and terrible day on Mount Calvary.

There is the promise of Heaven to those who live life in the shadow of the cross.

Chapter 4: When Blood Cries Out

In reading my Bible I have discovered that blood has a voice. It can speak. Look at Luke 11:50-51. Jesus rebukes the Pharisees and experts in the law. He said, "Woe unto you . . ." for a variety of their failings. And then He said:

"Therefore this generation will be held responsible for the blood of all the prophets that has been shed since the beginning of the world, from the blood of Abel to the blood of Zechariah, who was killed between the altar and the sanctuary. Yes, I tell you, this generation will be held responsible for it all."

He mentions the blood of all the prophets, the blood of Abel and the blood of Zechariah. And He tells them twice that they will be held accountable for this blood that was spilled. That is the context within which Jesus spoke. In order to understand the meaning of what He said, you have to go back and study the incidents He refers to in the lives of the men mentioned. Then the meaning becomes clearer, and we will see that blood has a voice, and it speaks. But what it says depends upon the one who has died.

In Genesis 4 we have the story of the first murder. The Book of Genesis is an interesting book. Genesis means "beginning". This book tells of the creation of our world;
    the first man
    the first family

the first flood
the beginning of the nation of Israel.
It has a lot of firsts in it.

It also, unfortunately has the first murder recorded in it. The first tribal wars, the first mass migration, and the beginnings of so many things – like music and art and the building of the first city are all found in the Book of Genesis, the book of beginnings.

The first murder is recorded in Genesis 4. Cain and Abel are sons of Adam and Eve. Both of them are raised with knowledge of God. They have been taught to offer sacrifices to the Lord as a way of worship. The scripture tells us that Abel was a farmer, and he brought the produce of his field as a gift to God. Cain was a shepherd. He brought a lamb to be slain as a sacrifice to the Lord. The Bible says in verse 4 that Abel's sacrifice was an acceptable one, and that he was favored by God as a result. But his brother Cain was jealous of him, and killed him (verse 8).

In verse 10, when the Lord is speaking with Cain about the death of his brother, scripture reads:

The Lord said, "What have you done? Listen! Your brother's blood cries out to me from the ground."

This is the first instance we have of blood speaking. Blood cried out from the ground.

Abel was an innocent man. He was brutally and savagely murdered by his own brother. Not because of something he said or did. He was killed out of jealous anger. Cain wanted what Abel had --

God's favor. Cain wanted God's blessing. Instead of changing his lifestyle and attitude to receive blessing and favor, he slew his brother instead.

No doubt he figured he would get away with it. I am sure he did it at a time when no one else was around. He probably figured his parents would ask after Abel. Cain could pretend he didn't know where his brother was. The truth would never be known. It would have been convenient for him if it had happened that way but it didn't because God knew. God had seen it all. He was a silent eyewitness to the whole thing.

"Listen!" the Lord commanded Cain. "Your brother's blood is crying out to me from the ground!"

Innocent blood had been spilled. Now the soil of the Earth was stained for the first time with a man's lifeblood. (Unfortunately, it would not be the last time.) That innocent blood had a voice. It cried out. What do you suppose it cried out for? What would innocent blood cry out to God for?

I submit that it cried out for vengeance!

I believe that his blood still cries out today. Still today, when innocent blood falls to the Earth it cries out to God against all murderers everywhere. And the cry is for vengeance!

"Avenge me, O Lord! I have been wronged! I have been murdered! My life was taken from me. I call out to you to avenge my death. You are the great judge! You balance all of life. Avenge me against those who took my life!"

God's response was to banish Cain from the area, and mark him so others would not slay him when they met him. Cain was made to wander on his own till the day he died.

When Abel's innocent blood was spilled, it cried out for vengeance.

Now let's look at this man, Zechariah. His story is found in 2 Chronicles 24. Zechariah was a priest, and a son of a holy priest named Jehoiada. His father, Jehoiada had been instrumental in leading the nation of Israel back into proper worship of the Lord. He had influence with their king, Joash. The temple was rebuilt, and the people all gave and served faithfully as they were supposed to. Unfortunately, when the priest, Jehoiada died, King Joash's counselors spoke with him, and soon he broke away from the Lord and allowed pagan worship to re-enter the country.

Jehoiada was gone, and did not see the backsliding of the nation. However in those days, the priesthood ran in families so his son, Zechariah saw it all. He was established as a priest, and served in the Temple when the worship of Baal and Asherah resumed. No doubt, it broke his heart. It grieved his spirit to see people forsake the living God and abandon themselves to idolatrous worship. All his righteous father worked for was destroyed. All that he had been raised to believe was holy and good was torn down and ignored.

The scripture tells us that God sent prophets to warn the people but they were ignored. (v. 19) When he could stand it no longer, Zechariah stood up. God anointed him with the Holy Spirit. He spoke out against idol worship. He spoke out against the lascivious living and the low standards that were in vogue.

Then the Spirit of God came upon Zechariah son of Jehoiada the priest. He stood before the people and said, "This is what God says: 'Why do you disobey the Lord's commands? You will not prosper. Because you have forsaken the LORD, he has forsaken you." (v. 20)

This so angered the people, that some of them plotted against him. The Bible tells us in verse 21 that they stoned him to death – by order of the king – in the courtyard of the Lord's temple. His dying words were: "May the Lord see this and call you into account!"

They spilled innocent blood on sacred ground. They killed a man – not because he was a criminal and deserved it. They murdered him because he was righteous and they were wicked. He stood up and spoke against the evil of his day as his father had. However, his father had held influence with the king, and a revival swept the nation. Now, Zechariah would pay with his life for his boldness and his commitment to the Lord.

He cried: "May the Lord see this and call you into account!"

His innocent blood, spilled by the hands of sinners on the sacred ground of the Temple, cried for God to intervene. "May the Lord call you into account!" In other words, "May the Lord deal with you as you have dealt with me." This is what he is saying. He wants God to deal with them, to confront them. He cries out to the Lord to address this wrong and make it right.

His blood cried out for vengeance, too!

And how did the Lord respond to this senseless slaughter of his faithful servant? We are told in vv. 23-25 that the Arameans attacked Israel and defeated them. Though they were a smaller army, the Lord delivered the soldiers of Israel into their hands. They wounded King Joash severely in the battle. As he lay dying on his bed, some of the leaders of Israel came and killed him.

Zechariah's innocent blood cried out from the Temple floor, calling for vengeance.

Now let's look at one more instance of an innocent man being murdered. For this, we search the New Testament. In the Gospel accounts of Matthew, Mark, Luke and John we find the story of Jesus' life, death and resurrection.

Like Abel and Zechariah before him, Jesus was a righteous man. In fact, He lived a sinless life. He was tested in all points as we are, and yet He never sinned. (Hebrews 4:15). He preached and demonstrated the power of the Kingdom of God. His teachings and these demonstrations so angered the religious leaders of His day that they conspired against Him and succeeded in having him executed through crucifixion.

And yet, while He hung there on the cross, the victim of jealousy, fear, anger and hatred, He

did not call down destruction on their heads as He could have. He could have
> rebuked them
> threatened them
> warned them

He could have called down a legion of angels to rescue Him and wipe them all out. He could have done so – but He did not. You see, that wasn't part of the plan. Nor was it in Jesus' nature to do so. Instead, the Bible tells us, He prayed for them. And this is what He prayed:

Then said Jesus, "Father, forgive them; for they know not what they do." (Luke 23:24)

Jesus – when He had an opportunity to speak about his persecutors – asked the Lord to *forgive* them. He understood that these people did not know what they were truly doing. Had they known who they were trying to kill, they would have stopped the execution immediately. But they didn't. They were blind. Jesus knew that. So He asked the Father to forgive them.

As the blood ran down that wooden cross, staining it forever with the precious blood of the Lamb of God, it fell to the ground, running down into the sand and soil below Him. And as it fell, do you know what it cried out for? Vengeance? No. Not vengeance.

No, Jesus' blood cried out for . . . mercy! "Mercy, Father. Forgive them, Father. Don't hold them accountable for this, Lord. Forgive them,

Lord. Pass over them. Do not bring judgment on them for this."

And do you know that His blood still speaks today? Yes, it does. His blood still cries out to the throne of God today. Do you believe me? Turn with me in your Bibles to Hebrews 12:24.

. . . to Jesus -- the mediator of a new covenant, and to the sprinkled blood that speaks a better word than the blood of Abel.

When Jesus died, He entered into the Temple of God in Heaven, and as High Priest He sprinkled His blood on the mercy seat of the Ark. By so doing, He was acting as our great High Priest, our intermediary, our go-between making atonement for the sins of His people once and for all. Hallelujah!

The writer of Hebrews tells us that Jesus' blood speaks a better word than Abel's blood. Both men were innocent. Both were righteous. Both were senselessly murdered.

The difference between the two?

Abel's blood (like Zechariah's) cried out for vengeance, and the Lord executed judgment on their killers. But Jesus' blood cried out for mercy – a stay of execution.

What was God's response? He forgave them. He showed grace and mercy toward them.

When Jesus asked God to forgive them, He meant it for us as well. The Father spared them. He agreed to work with them and bring them into fellowship with Himself. He does the same for us, too.

Today Jesus' blood cries out for mercy, for grace, for forgiveness of your sins. We must seize this moment to not only be forgiven but also to learn to love like Jesus loves.

To forgive as the Father forgives.

To show mercy when others choose judgment.

To choose peace when others want to fight.

To be silent when others rage.

To learn to ask God to forgive those who hurt us so our blood – like the precious blood of the Lamb's – will cry for mercy and not for vengeance.

Jesus' blood cries out for mercy. May He cover you with His.

Chapter 5: It Wasn't the Cross that Killed Jesus

When we share the Lord's Supper, we do so to remember what Jesus accomplished for us on the cross. Had He not gone and died there in our place, salvation would not have been purchased for us. None of us would be saved. The price of redemption was a blood sacrifice from a pure lamb, a holy lamb, and God provided that faithful lamb when He sent Jesus to hang on the cross.

When I became a Christian, I read the Gospel story. Honestly, I felt the ending was a terrible tragedy. I read the crucifixion scene in all four gospel accounts. Each time I did, I was struck with immense sadness. I didn't see celebration. I didn't see victory. I had to study a lot and listen to my preacher to understand that what Jesus accomplished by going to the cross was all part of God's plan; not only God's plan for Jesus' life but also God's plan for our lives, too. To me it was a tragedy. Jesus was the hero. Since He suffered and died, I expected a bad guy. I was looking for a villain. That's how we read fiction or other stories we encounter -- whether on television or in the movies or maybe in stories we are told. There is always a good guy and a bad guy. And if the good guy is suffering, we know it is the bad guy's fault, right? The bad guy is responsible for all the suffering in the story.

So when I read how Jesus suffered, died and was buried, I was looking for a bad guy. I needed a villain to pin all of my hatred on. I carefully combed through the scriptures looking to see who exactly was responsible for Jesus' suffering and death. I needed a "wanted" poster like they used in the Old West. They would print a wanted poster, and display it offering a reward for the kill or capture of the villain.

"Wanted: Dead or Alive".

As I went through scripture, several names popped out. I knew with such a bad group of guys, it would be easy to find who was responsible.

First, there was Herod.

A governor that could have helped Jesus but chose not to do anything. He didn't want to deal with Him. He didn't help Him and by not helping Him, he hurt Him so Herod was definitely one of the bad guys.

Another villain was Annas.

He was the high priest, and he didn't like Jesus. (He was jealous of Jesus and felt threatened by His abilities and popularity.) Of all the priests, he was the high priest. He must have been looked up to and admired. He probably liked that. Most of us would. Here is a guy that dedicated himself to serving the Lord all the days of his life. He works hard and does all the right things. He's probably politically motivated so he wheels and deals and eventually makes it to the top. He becomes the high priest. He's the number one guy. Unfortunately, he's jealous of Jesus because Jesus has got this fantastic ministry going. He's healing the sick, cleansing the lepers, raising the dead. He's saying things the people have never heard, and teaching things in a bold way, not like the priests. So He's got a following. He's only been around a few years, and he's got more people talking about Him and following Him that Annas has ever had. That had to bother Annas a great deal. Early on we're told Annas and Caiaphas got together with the Sanhedrin, and started plotting to get rid of Jesus. If they couldn't ruin His reputation, then they would have Him killed. That's strange. The high priests and the religious leaders are plotting to kill a prophet that's bugging them. Isn't that weird?

Speaking of Caiaphas, he's another bad guy.

In the Old Testament, when God was spoke to the Jews through Moses, He told them they would have a high priest, and every year that priest would change. When you read the Gospel accounts, the writers refer to Annas *and* Caiaphas as high priests.

How does that happen? How did they get two?

Do some research, and you'll find they were related! This is really fishy, and as they play their roles they stink to high Heaven. Caiaphas isn't any good either. He's another bad guy. He's locked in step with Annas. Annas wants Jesus dealt with and so does Caiaphas. Annas says, "Jesus has to go," and Caiaphas is in agreement. So Caiaphas is our third villain.

They were over the Sanhedrin. The Sanhedrin was an organization of religious scholars who had tremendous influence over the Jewish people. They were opposed to Jesus as well. These were supposed to be the most religious people around. They studied the Old Testament. They were waiting for the Messiah to come. They taught in the synagogues, and trained all the kids in the Jewish faith. And yet these are the very guys that were disturbed by Jesus. They wanted him out of the way.

Some of it was jealousy. They didn't have the popularity Jesus did. But some of it was fear. They were afraid of what the Roman government would do if too many people got behind Jesus. What if the commoners wanted to make Him king? The Sanhedrin knew the Romans wouldn't stand by and let that go on. There was no king allowed but Caesar in Rome. Any upstarts were seen as rebels and would be dealt with accordingly.

So the members of the Sanhedrin are bad guys, too. Some plotted against Jesus. Others let them plot and did nothing. Not all of them were bad. Most of them did nothing but side with Annas and Caiaphas when they wanted to kill Jesus. However, there were a few who knew there was something special about Him.

In John 3, we read where Nicodemus was a member of the Sanhedrin. He came to Jesus in the night so he would not be seen. He snuck over secretly. Why? He didn't want his fellow priests, lawyers and doctors of the law to know he was speaking with the enemy. Keep in mind this is early on in the story. This is John 3. Jesus is not going to get into trouble until about 19-20 chapters later. But it is interesting that Nicodemus comes to him in the night.

Listen to what he says: "Master, we know you are from God, for no man could do the things you do unless God was with him." (v. 2)

Listen to that! First, he uses the word "we". That means he wasn't alone in his belief that God was working with Jesus. He knew God had sent Jesus. He wasn't saying he believed Jesus was the Messiah. He was saying that he recognized the hand of God on Jesus' life and ministry. And not just him. He said "we". Which means there were other members who detected a divine touch on Jesus' life.

Second, he says he knows that Jesus is sent from God. In other words, he was probably at the point where he suspected Jesus was a true prophet. How does he know that God is working with Jesus? He has seen with his eyes and heard with his ears what Jesus is doing for people. For him to say, "No man could do the things you do unless God was working with him" means that Nicodemus was aware of the miracles, healings and deliverances that were taking place.

Don't be confused about the "master". When he called him master, he wasn't acknowledging Jesus' divinity. That was a title. In some translations, he calls him "rabbi", another word for "teacher". In other words, he acknowledged Jesus was a teacher when he called him "master". He wasn't calling him Lord.

So Nicodemus reveals that not all of the Sanhedrin desired Jesus' death. Many of them did. The ones that weren't were a minority in the group. None of them spoke up and defended Him when they had the chance to do so. So you have to look at the Sanhedrin as bad guys, too.

How about Pontius Pilate?

Pontius was a governor sent from Rome. He had nothing personal against Jesus. He was more like a soldier or a politician just following orders or obeying the law as he saw it. When you read the accounts of his interactions with the Jewish leaders about Jesus, you see that he didn't want to deal with Him. His wife had had a bad dream and warned him not to have anything to do with Jesus. (Matt. 27:19) Pilate doesn't have it in for Jesus. In fact, he tries to reason with the Jewish leaders to just run Him off and forget about Him. Unfortunately by this time, Satan had the Sanhedrin on a roll. There was no way they were going to give up and walk away. They were determined to see Jesus die.

So Pilate argues, reasons and sends Him away. When they bring Him back from Herod, he has Him whipped. But none of it is enough.

The Jews want death, and Pilate gives them one. First though, he washes his hands, claiming he is innocent of the Lord's blood. A futile gesture but indicative of Pilate's feelings about Jesus' guilt or innocence. I am not sure what was going through Pilate's mind at the time. But because he chose not to spare Jesus' life and chose instead to condemn him to die as the Jewish leaders wanted, we have to label him as a bad guy, too.

So on the Villain List, you've got:
Annas, the high priest
Caiaphas, the other high priest
the Sanhedrin
Governor Herod
Pontius Pilate

That's a lot of wanted posters. If you're looking for bad guys, the scriptures give you plenty to choose from.

On the other side, you've got Jesus and his disciples. Unfortunately, the disciples run away when the bad guys show up. So really, you've got Jesus on his own facing the bad guys down by Himself.

Were the Jews responsible for killing Jesus? Were the Roman soldiers who were responsible for the actual crucifixion? Can we blame Annas and Caiaphas? Can we hang it all on Herod or Pilate?

That would be neat and tidy if we could. To be honest however, we can't really make any of them the bad guys. The truth is that it wasn't any of the men mentioned that were responsible for killing the Lord.

We're told that there were nails driven into Jesus as He hung on the cross. Two would have been driven into his hands (or wrists), and another would have been driven into his feet after his ankles were crossed. Three iron nails, driven through flesh and bone and into wood.

In fact, the law requires that nearly everything be cleansed with blood, and without the shedding of blood there is no forgiveness. (Hebrew 9:22)

Someone had to die. God could not forgive us unless someone shed his blood for us. So Jesus went to the cross when it should have been us. **He took our place.** I want you to get that. By all rights, it should have been you on that cross. It should have been me. We were the sinners. We were the guilty ones. The Bible tells us that Jesus was sinless. He had no business being there. But He deliberately surrendered his life on our behalf. Jesus died for you. He died for you so you could live for Him.

FIRST NAIL – GOD'S JUSTICE

The first nail they drove into Jesus represented God's justice. God's justice called for someone to die. God made us with certain expectations for our behavior. As soon as we could, we broke the law. When there was only one rule in the Garden of Eden, we broke the rule. So we were the sinners. We were the ones who broke God's law, and His law demanded justice.

Before the Lord ever gave the Law to Moses, He instituted blood sacrifice for sin on our part. Do you remember when God told Adam and Eve not to eat the fruit from the Tree of the Knowledge of Good and Evil? But they did anyway, didn't they? They broke the only law in the book! The scripture tells us that they were ashamed because they became aware of their nakedness. So the Lord brought them animal skins to wear. Where do you think he got the animal skins?

I'll tell you where: He had to take the life of one of the animals He had created in order to provide skins for Adam and Eve to wear.

A blood sacrifice was made for our parents in the Garden of Eden. And it was done by the Lawgiver's hand.

In Hebrews 4:15 it is written:

For we do not have a high priest who is unable to sympathize with our weaknesses, but we have one who has been tempted in every way, just as we are—yet was without sin.

Jesus was without sin. The sinless one took the fall for all the sinners in the world. **The blameless one died so the ones who deserved all the blame could live.** The Lord of Light stepped into shadow so the children of darkness could run into the sun. You've got to get this picture. It is crucial to your understanding what happened at Calvary. Jesus was without sin. But His great love for you drove Him to the cross. His affection for you helped Him carry it. His passion for you helped him endure that dark night of His arrest and trial. His desire for you made Him climb that hill.

Jesus was holy. He was pure. He was untainted with sin. He had a human nature but He did not have a sinful nature. He was consecrated to the Lord, wholly given over to the service of God. He was set apart for special use in the Father's Kingdom.

SECOND NAIL – JESUS' LOVE

Jesus elected to do what He knew you and I could not do. He chose to take our place because He knew we were unable, unwilling and disqualified to hang there. The law required a perfect lamb without blemish.

But our sin blemishes us. Our sin stains us.

Although we deserved the death penalty, our sin hindered us from hanging there and dying to pay that awful price. Thank God for Jesus. The perfect Lamb of God who came to take away the sin of the world was able to do it! (John 1:29)

We couldn't. But He could.

We didn't. But He did.

Jesus, moved with compassion, became the sacrifice the law demanded.

"Greater love has no one than this that he lay down his life for his friends." (John 15:13)

The first nail represents God's Justice. The second nail represents Jesus' great Love for us. Now we arrive at the third and final nail. That third nail represents our sin. Pay close attention, please . . .

THIRD NAIL – OUR SIN

You and I have fallen from grace. We have sinned. In fact, we are all born into sin, and we keep sinning as long as we are human.

For all have sinned and fallen short of the glory of God. (Romans 3:23)

All of us have missed the mark. All of us have fallen short. All of us fail God. Compared to His perfection and glory, we don't even register on the chart. You can't compare us with God. You can only contrast us in our fallen state.

Our sin has broken God's law. Our iniquity stains us. Our transgressions mark us. We carry our "wrong" with us like a brand. It separates us from fellowship with the Father.

The Bible instructs us in Romans 6:23:

Now the wages of sin is death but the gift of God is eternal life through Jesus Christ our Lord.

Wages are what we get paid. The payment for sinning against God is death! We have death waiting for us because of our sin. That death - in the spiritual sense - means eternal separation from the Lord. God did not make you to live apart from Him for all eternity. He made you to have a relationship with you. He brings us into His house to live with Him forever. (John 14:3)

Knowing our sin separates us from Him, and sin leads to death which means being forever separated from Him, He had to create a way for us to bridge that gap so we could be restored to a proper relationship with him. A sacrifice had to be made on our behalf. Since none of us were clean or holy enough to do it, He had to put His own dear son to death, and do it for us.

> He made a door named Jesus,
> and then opened the door for us.
>
> He made a bridge,
> and then crossed over it to get us.
>
> He devised a plan
> because we could not.
>
> He made the sacrifice
> because we would not.
>
> He paid the price
> because we were broke.
>
> He took the beating

because He knew we couldn't take it.

So this wonderful exchange took place:
Jesus, the Lord of Life laid down His life and accepted a shroud of death so we might get up out of our spiritual graves, and put on His robe of light, His robe of righteousness.

He died so we could live.
He suffered so we could go free.
All we had to offer was sin and death. He took that away - our sin and the death that goes with it - and gave us instead righteousness and life.
In light of that knowledge, our perspective changes a bit. I was looking for a bad guy, a wanted poster. I wanted someone to hang this terrible crime on. Instead, what I find is three nails.
God's justice.
Jesus' love.
And my sin.
None of those sound like Caiaphas or Annas, do they? None of those sound like Pontius or Herod, do they? No, they don't. The reason is because the fellows I named (even though none of them were innocent), were all minor players in this great cosmic drama that unfolds in the gospel story. All of them have a brief opportunity to be center stage.
But **God's justice** drove Jesus to Calvary.
Jesus' love made Him carry that cross on our behalf.

Lastly, it was **our sin** that hung Him on that tree.

It wasn't the cross that killed Jesus, beloved. It was our sin.

And it was God's life-giving power that raised Him from the dead!

Chapter 6: The Cry of the Centurion

And when the centurion, who stood there in front of Jesus, heard his cry and saw how he died, he said, "Surely this man was the Son of God!"
(Mark 15:39)

Picture Calvary in your mind. There on the hill are three rough, wooden crosses. There are three men hanging on them. The scriptures tell us Jesus hung in the middle between the two. The other two crosses held two thieves condemned to die. There was a crowd of people on the hill surrounding the crosses. Some of them were laughing, pointing and heckling the three dying men. Others stared in shock and awe, amazed at the barbarous cruelty they witnessed. Others were there to cry and mourn; family members and friends of the condemned.

I am sure there were more rocks and dirt than grass or flowers. I am sure it was not a pleasant place to visit. No doubt the people in attendance had been there before. They knew the way up the hill. They knew what took place there. They'd seen other hapless souls killed on the crosses. That didn't make it any easier. We don't know what sort of day it was. Was the sun shining or was it overcast? Was it hot? Did it matter? Calvary was a place of death. It would be for us today like going into a gas chamber or visiting the electric chair. Imagine standing in the small room in prison where they give lethal injections to murderers. Calvary was a place where the condemned went to die. The Roman soldiers went about their jobs with cruel and casual precision. The wailers cried and mourned. Family members and friends hung their heads, wringing their hands, hopeless to do anything for their loved ones.

But on that hill that sad, terrible day, an amazing thing happened. A man who didn't know God, an ordinary centurion, a soldier in the Roman army made an incredible discovery and voiced an astounding statement. His words were few but they have had a lasting impact on eternity.

First, he had an inspiration from God, followed by a revelation from the Holy Spirit, and then a bold confession that changed his life forever.

Inspiration

When the Lord reaches out to our lives, He reaches out to touch us. We use the word *inspire* to mean:
    a. to influence
    b. to move or to guide someone by divine or supernatural force

In scripture, it means:
    a. to breathe or blow upon
    b. to breathe life into or infuse with energy

The word "breath" in Greek is *pneuma* which can mean *breath* or *spirit*.

The Holy Spirit breathed upon this man, and he was infused with the power of God – enough to proclaim: "Surely this man was the Son of God!"

The Lord wants to blow upon us. He wants to blow His breath on us and inspire us, to infuse us with energy. He wants to use His divine influence to move us closer to Himself for a deeper revelation of who He is and what He is doing in our world. He wants to move us closer to one another as well and share His love.

Listen to how Elijah was inspired by the Lord one time when he was alone and lonely.

There he went into a cave and spent the night. And the word of the LORD came to him: "What are you doing here, Elijah?"

He replied, "I have been very zealous for the LORD God Almighty. The Israelites have rejected your covenant, broken down your altars, and put your prophets to death with the sword. I am the only one left, and now they are trying to kill me too."

The LORD said, "Go out and stand on the mountain in the presence of the LORD, for the LORD is about to pass by."

Then a great and powerful wind tore the mountains apart and shattered the rocks before the LORD, but the LORD was not in the wind. After the wind there was an earthquake, but the LORD was not in the earthquake. After the earthquake came a fire, but the LORD was not in the fire. And after the fire came a gentle whisper. When Elijah heard it, he pulled his cloak over his face and went out and stood at the mouth of the cave. (I Kings 19:9-13)

Sometimes the Lord will come to us in a bold and dramatic way. Maybe it's a powerful wind or an earthquake. Maybe He will come like fire. Other times He comes in a gentle voice, a quiet whisper, like He did with Elijah.

Regardless how He chooses to come, He has a fresh word for us today if we will only listen. And His word is guaranteed to *inspire* us.

Revelation

Jesus had told His disciples earlier that only God can reveal the Lordship of Christ to people. It comes through divine revelation.

"But what about you?" He asked. "Who do you say I am?"
Simon Peter answered, "You are the Christ, the Son of the living God."
Jesus replied, "Blessed are you, Simon son of Jonah, for this was not revealed to you by man, but by my Father in Heaven." (Matt. 16:15-17)

Only God's Holy Spirit can reveal Jesus to us. Man can't. The same Holy Spirit that showed Peter that Jesus was the Christ is the same Holy Spirit that showed the centurion at the cross that Jesus was the Son of God. It is when the Lord removes our blinders and allows us to perceive things supernaturally that we can see Christ for who He truly is.

Some may say "Didn't the day turning to night alert him?"

But that alone would not necessarily make the centurion think Jesus' claims were true. He may have seen an eclipse before or perhaps heard of one.

"What about the veil in the temple ripping in two when He died? Wouldn't that have alerted him to Jesus' supernatural lineage?"

No, the temple was back in the city. They were outside the city walls on a hill. There was no way the centurion could have known that was happening.

Almighty God divinely breathed on this man, and revealed the truth to him, that here before him -- the man on the cross who had just given up the ghost -- was the very Son of God.

We have to have a supernatural revelation to come to know God, to recognize Jesus for who He truly is. It must be a personal experience. We can't know Him because of what someone else told us. When the Lord shows you Christ for who He really is, then you can say: "I know it in my knower. I know it way down on the inside. Now, I am completely convinced that He is who He says He is and that He can do what He says He can do."

We need a supernatural experience, a divine manifestation to believe and confess it boldly. As we sing in *Amazing Grace*: "How precious did that grace appear the hour I first believed."

Jonah didn't believe he needed to listen to God when the Lord called him. He ran. But God found him. The Lord allowed him to be thrown overboard into a raging sea where he was swallowed by a fish. The Bible tells us Jonah was in the belly of the fish for three days. I don't know about you, but I would been convinced it was time to listen to God the *first* day. Certainly by the second! But it took Jonah three days to surrender and say, "Here I am, Lord. You've got my attention. What would you like me to do?"

From that point on, I bet Jonah never ignored God again!

When Daniel was thrown into the den of lions the soldiers thought they would find him dead and eaten the next day. That evening God sent an angel to shut the mouths of the lions so Daniel was safe. Imagine the guard's surprise the next morning when they looked into the pit and saw Daniel well-rested and eager to speak with the king! Do you think that Daniel ever doubted that the Lord could do anything after that?

These two men experienced the power of God in a miraculous way. When the Lord revealed Himself to them, when He showed them what He was capable of doing, it strengthened their testimony. It made them bolder witnesses for Him. They realized they were serving a supernatural God with divine power.

That's the way He works with us, too. He inspires us through His Holy Spirit. When He reveals things to us, when we get a fresh revelation of who God is and what He is capable of doing, it emboldens us and makes our testimony sure. We're able to say, "Surely, Jesus is the Son of God" because we too have the power of God illuminating that truth to our souls.

It starts with inspiration. Then we are moved to revelation. That inspiring fire moves us to a point of confession.

Confession

The centurion confessed: "Surely, this man was the Son of God."

He acknowledged Jesus for who He was because he understood what others had seen. God mercifully opened his eyes and allowed him to pierce through his spiritual darkness to see a truth that had been hidden from him.

He didn't figure it out. We can't figure it out. If we could look at Jesus long enough and eventually figure out who He is, then He would not have had to go to the cross and die in our place. He would not have had to suffer as He did. Christianity would be a game of mental science. The smartest folks would get to go to Heaven, and leave the rest of us behind. Surprisingly, the Lord doesn't necessarily want brainy kids so much as He wants children who love Him and appreciate what He has done for them. Christianity isn't a science project. It isn't a logic test. More than the head, the Lord tends to go for your heart. The Bible doesn't proclaim Him as "God is smart." It says, "God is love."

When the Lord reveals Jesus to us as our Christ, then we too, like the centurion on that dark hill, must make the same confession. Paul wrote:

That if you confess with your mouth, "Jesus is Lord," and believe in your heart that God raised

him from the dead, you will be saved. For it is with your heart that you believe and are justified, and it is with your mouth that you confess and are saved.
(Rom. 10:9-10)

    We will be inspired by His revelation to confess with boldness: "He is the Son of God. He is our Lord!" We have more evidence than the centurion did on that afternoon on Calvary.

We have the Holy Bible.

We have the Holy Spirit.

We have 2,000 years of Church history.

We should rise in holy boldness and add our voice to the cry of the centurion:

"SURELY,

THIS MAN JESUS

IS THE SON OF GOD!"

Chapter 7: Let Us Go and Die with Him

I am crucified with Christ and I no longer live, but Christ lives in me. The life I live in the body, I live by faith in the Son of God, who loved me and gave himself for me. (Gal. 2:20)

Paul wrote this in a letter to the church in Galatia, calling them to a deeper walk in Christ. What he was saying was: "It is not enough to just know Christ for who He is or for what He has done. Just as Christ was crucified on the cross of Calvary, so we too must die to ourselves. We must crucify our flesh with its carnal mindset and worldly desires. We die to ourselves so that we no longer live life the way we want to but we live as if Christ was living His life through us."

It calls for a surrender of oneself, a bowing down and submission to His lordship over our lives. It is no longer what I want or what I think. What is more important is what He wants and what He thinks. **It is not my will but His will that must be done – both in and through me.**

This is what God calls us to. Christianity is symbolized by the cross for a reason. It represents death. Death on a cross. The Lord holds it up as a symbol of what Christ has done, and as a reminder: *we must die to ourselves*. We need to die to our sinful nature, to the things that lure us away from Him. He wants us to use the cross to put our flesh to death. Not to kill ourselves but to kill that part of us that wars against His Holy Spirit. This is what the Lord expects of us.

For if you live according to the sinful nature, you will die; but if by the Spirit you put to death the misdeeds of the body, you will live. (Rom. 8:13)

The Holy Spirit helps us kill our misdeeds. In the King James Version of the Bible, it is written: "... mortify [or kill] the flesh ..." meaning the sin nature. We must die to ourselves.

No, I beat my body and make it my slave so that after I have preached to others, I myself will not be disqualified for the prize. (I Cor. 9:27)

When he said, "I beat my body", he did not mean to make a whip and strike yourself as some have interpreted it. He means to bring yourself under control.

Control your thoughts.
Control your feelings.
Control your attitude.
"How?" you ask.
By filling your mind with the Word of God. So fill your thoughts with the Lord's thoughts that there won't be enough room in your life for all the other junk.

If the devil could, he would dominate and control your thoughts. He would fill you with thoughts of doom and gloom. He would fill you with depression and despair. He would fill you with darkness, clouds, smoke, a feeling of utter hopelessness and rejection. But he cannot. He cannot control your thoughts. Paul told Timothy who controls our minds.

For God has not given us the spirit of fear; but of power, and of love, and of a sound mind.
(2 Tim. 1:7)

God has given us a spirit of power. A spirit filled with love that we can share with others. He's given us control over our minds. He said we have the spirit of a sound mind.

A whole mind.
A well mind.
A healthy mind. Hallelujah!

Now, some people may not have a good mind. Some people are sick. They think evil thoughts and can't seem to stop. These people are oppressed by the devil. They have allowed evil spirits to come into their lives because they have entertained bad thoughts and dwelled on them. Now those bad thoughts have taken up residence in their minds. They have come to dominate that person's thought life.

Paul is not referring to those people in this scripture. Paul is writing to believers. Timothy was saved, like you are. He was born again, like you. He loved God the way you do. He worshipped the Lord like you and I. He told Timothy, "The Spirit of God has given you a sound (stable, solid, reliable and dependable) mind." Hallelujah!

When you fill your mind with the Word of God through reading

studying
listening to Bible-based messages
and prayer,
there won't be room for the devil's thoughts.

When you get busy doing the Lord's work, your time for the devil shrinks enormously. When you apply God's Word to your life, the Holy Spirit inside you kills off those things that displease God.

You'll be amazed at the freedom you'll enjoy. You'll hear the voice of the Lord better than ever. You'll see the hand of God working in your life and in other people's lives as well. Unexpected circumstances and coincidences will take shape, and you'll realize the unseen hand of the Lord is orchestrating wonderful things in your life!

Praise God!

Paul knew that this world, our flesh and the devil would work together to destroy and distract us from fulfilling God's purpose here on Earth. They conspire together. If it's not the world, then it is the flesh. If it is not the flesh, then it is the devil. Sometimes, it's a combination of the two. Sometimes, the devil teams up with the world and attacks us. Or our flesh will conspire with the devil to distract us.

That is why it is so important to be vigilant. We must be strong. We must be aware of what is going on around us. We are at war! Christianity is a war zone. You and I were born in the midst of a battle. Every day, we walk as children of light in a dark world. It seeks our ruin and destruction. So we're in a fight. The flesh works with the devil to be seduced by the world. Our spirit must rise up and overcome. Our spirit:

- must be fed daily the Word of God
- be filled with God's Holy Spirit
- bathed in His anointing

so we can defeat the devil and his demon forces.

The Lord knows a dead man can't be tempted. Amen? You'll never see a dead alcoholic rise up out of the grave and reach for a bottle of booze. A dead man never craned his neck to look at a pretty girl pass by. There has never been a dead junkie say out loud: "Man, I just wish I could get one more fix!"

The dead are beyond temptation. Isn't that right? Have you ever seen a corpse in a coffin at a funeral enjoying one last puff on a cigarette?

No, you haven't! And you never will! Why?

Because the dead are dead. All the tempting is over in their lives. All the temptations of this world are gone. The flesh doesn't matter. The world doesn't matter. The devil doesn't count. He's got no business with the dead. That's history. The dead are beyond temptation, beyond choice, beyond any appeal or seductive lure of anything.

God knows that if we crucify our sinful nature, if we put ourselves on an altar and slay the carnal man with the cross of Christ, then we will be dead to sin, too! We'll die to lustful temptations.

That temptation to shop till you're broke.
That temptation to eat till you're stuffed.

God isn't honored when we live that way. He doesn't want us living according to our sinful passions. I'm talking to the man who can't stop gambling, and to the woman who can't stop gossiping. That sort of behavior brings no honor to the Lord. You say you're His children -- but you act like you belong to the devil when your flesh runs your life. You look more like you belong to the world than to God when sins control you. If your habit makes you behave in a way that would be displeasing to the Lord, how can you win anyone to Jesus? How can you testify to His goodness and grace if your carnal man rules over your spirit man?

So, Paul tells us we must die to ourselves. And let me tell you: IT'S NOT EASY. It will take everything that is within you to live the life God wants you to live. Even then you cannot do it alone.

One of the most frustrating days of my life also became one of the most glorious days in my life when I realized I did not have it in me to live the life God was calling me to live.

God calls us to be holy, even as He is holy. (I Pet. 1:16) But we can't live a holy life. I tried but I couldn't do it.

I denied myself.	I took up my cross.
I prayed.	I fasted.
I read.	I studied.
I went to church.	I ministered to people.

But I couldn't live the life He wanted me to live. I kept slipping into sinful thoughts, words and actions. Finally, in desperation, I gave up and cried out to the Lord: "I can't do this! I can't be holy!"

It was then the Lord showed me that in and of myself I am incapable of being holy. If I could do it on my own I would have no need for Christ and His cross. (John 15:5) Then He showed me that if I die to myself, let the cross do its work in me and allow His Holy Spirit to live through me, it would be easier. In other words, the Lord said: "Get out of the way, and let me drive!"

Once I did that – once I surrendered to His leadership -- my walk with the Lord got a *lot* easier. That was when I realized I couldn't -- but He could!

Hallelujah!

I can't -- but He can! Praise God!

Do you see how it works? God has called us to live our lives in a way that is above and beyond our human capability to do so. So we must give up trying and give in to His leadership -- allow Him to take over – so He lives His life through us, and we go along for the ride!

I tell people: "Any good you see in me is Jesus' fault. I am responsible for everything else." In fact, when I get down and depressed, it is usually because I am trying to take on something I can't handle. I am trying to do God's job. When I surrender, when I give up and let Him take over, everything works better and peace returns to me.

When Paul wrote: "I no longer live but Christ lives in me" this is what he was talking about. He had stepped aside and allowed Jesus to live through him. This is what brings us into fellowship with God. This is where we find the unity, bonding and closeness that we desire. God desires it, too.

You will never feel as close to God as you will the day you die to self and let Jesus live through you.

Man, that's power! And, it is peace!
You have got to die to yourself in order to enter into life with God.

Now a man named Lazarus was sick. He was from Bethany, the village of Mary and her sister Martha. This Mary, whose brother Lazarus now lay sick, was the same one who poured perfume on the Lord and wiped his feet with her hair. So the *sisters sent word to Jesus, "Lord, the one you love is sick."*

When he heard this, Jesus said, "This sickness will not end in death. No, it is for God's glory so that God's Son may be glorified through it." Jesus loved Martha and her sister and Lazarus. Yet when he heard that Lazarus was sick, he stayed where he was two more days. Then he said to his disciples, "Let us go back to Judea."

"But Rabbi," they said, "a short while ago the Jews tried to stone you, and yet you are going back there?"

Jesus answered, "Are there not twelve hours of daylight? A man who walks by day will not stumble, for he sees by this world's light. It is when he walks by night that he stumbles, for he has no light." After he had said this, he went on to tell them, "Our friend Lazarus has fallen asleep; but I am going there to wake him up."

His disciples replied, "Lord, if he sleeps, he will get better." Jesus had been speaking of his death, but his disciples thought he meant natural sleep.

So then he told them plainly, "Lazarus is dead, and for your sake I am glad I was not there, so that you may believe. But let us go to him."

Then Thomas (called Didymus) said to the rest of the disciples, "Let us also go, that we may die with him." (John 11:1-16)

Lazarus died and was buried. When Jesus brought him back to life, he was a different man. You would be, too! No one dies and is brought back to life by the hand of God and acts the same way. Can you imagine the testimony he gave?

"Well, one morning I woke up, and I didn't feel very good. As the day wore on, I got sicker and finally I laid down and died. Then a few days later, just before my sisters were going to bury me, Jesus came and brought me back to life. Now, I feel a lot better!"

If you are follower of Jesus Christ, get ready because one day you will be able to testify to the same thing. "I died -- but Jesus brought me back to life!" Hallelujah!

There have been many people down through history who have died and come back to life and testified to what they have seen and heard on the other side. Some talk about Heaven. Some talk about Hell. Some talk about seeing dead relatives. Some claim to see and speak with Jesus or with an angel. Although some of their stories are different, the bottom line is this: there is an unseen world beyond this one, a spirit world where we are all bound. We will determine here on Earth whether we spend eternity in Heaven or Hell.

Lazarus is an example of physical death. But there are other kinds of death as well. For some, it means the death of a dream.

"Lord," Martha said to Jesus, "if you had been here, my brother would not have died."
(John 11: 21)

Mary and Martha both had a dream, a wish for their sick brother, Lazarus. They wanted him to get better. They wanted him well. They wanted him healed and healthy. But he was sick, and dying. I am sure they tried every medicine they could get afford. You would too if your brother was sick and dying. You would do everything you could to make him comfortable. They probably traveled the entire city in search of a cure. They loved their brother, and did not want to see him suffer.

They had hope though. They all three knew Jesus. They had heard him preach and teach. They had seen Him heal sick people. The ladies thought: "If only Jesus was here. Jesus heals people all the time. He could speak a word, and Lazarus would get well!"

No doubt they were praying that He would come and save their brother from death. They sent a messenger to go find him and ask him to come quickly before they lost Lazarus.

The story tells us Jesus delayed when He heard the news. He tarried. He was in no hurry to get there. He didn't seem too concerned that Lazarus was sick and about to die.

When He arrived, Martha said: "If you had been here, my brother would not have died."

They had a dream, a hope that Lazarus could get better when Jesus touched him. But Jesus wasn't there. Their brother did not get better. He got sicker, and then he died. And their dream died with him. So when Jesus arrived four days after he expired, they were heart-broken. Not only was their brother dead but their dream of sharing more years with him had died, too.

Back in those days, the man worked to support the women in the family. Because no mention is made of Mary or Martha having a husband to support them, we assume they were single, perhaps widowed. Which means Lazarus, their brother was the bread-winner in the family. Their financial future depended on him. When he died, their future prosperity looked bleak. So their dream of continuing on was gone. They didn't see much hope for tomorrow.

Maybe your dream has died in you. Maybe something you hoped for is gone now and there doesn't seem to be a way to ever attain it. What I say to you is:

"Don't ever give up! As long as Jesus is on the throne, all things are possible."

That which is impossible to man is possible with God. (Luke 18:27)

The dream you once had can be brought back to life just like Lazarus was brought back to life from death.

Jesus isn't stumped by anyone's death. He doesn't throw in the towel just because someone or something dies. No, He goes forward because He has a plan. It is a good plan. It's one that will work. He does not always reveal every part of the plan to us. But we know that He loves us and wants what is best for us. So momentary hurts and pains scar us, sure. We think sometimes we are looking at the end of the world because some business fails or because some relationship ends.

Don't give up. Don't throw in the towel. God is still working! This isn't the end of the road. It is just a bend in the road. He isn't finished yet.

We Must Die with Him

If we want to enter into intimate fellowship with God, we must be resolutely determined to die. See the picture . . .

Lazarus, a close friend of the Lord's is dead. His sisters and their friends are filled with grief over his loss. They are in mourning. Mary and Martha are upset. Their brother is gone. Their companion has left. Their provider is absent.

There is more trouble, too. This is not necessarily a safe place for Jesus to be. Remember when Thomas said in verse 16:

"Come, let us go with him that we may die also"?

The reason he said that is because the last time they were in Bethany, Jesus made the Jews mad with His preaching and teaching and they tried to stone Him. The word was out that the Galilean was a heretic and worthy of death. So He left them with a bad feeling. They were determined that if He came back into their town again, they were going to kill Him by stoning Him to death. It naturally followed they would kill his disciples who were with Him as well because they believed His teachings. So Bethany was not a good place to be. It certainly was not safe or inviting for Jesus and his followers.

"I tell you the truth," Jesus answered, "before Abraham was born, I am!" At this, they picked up stones to stone him, but Jesus hid himself, slipping away from the temple grounds. (John 8:58-59)

Yes, He had run into some trouble with the Jews in Bethany before. Now He was re-entering the war zone, that hostile territory to see Mary and Martha. The disciples were a bit confused. They remembered the Jews being angry. They knew the stones were still hard. They knew they would be recognized.

Let me tell you: when you serve the Lord and sell out to Him to follow Him whole-heartedly, there will be times when you will be confused. There will be times when His leading doesn't make sense. You may experience turmoil and tension. You'll get worried, and maybe even fearful. You'll suffer anxious thoughts when trouble comes.

Listen! One thing will hold you. It is found in Galatians 2:20, the very scripture verse we started with.

I have been crucified with Christ and I no longer live, but Christ lives in me. The life I live in the body, I live by faith in the Son of God, who loved me and gave himself for me.

Jesus loves you, and He gave Himself for you. If you have crucified your life, then you no longer live. It is Christ that lives in you. And the life you now live, you live by faith in the Son of God.

It is Christ who causes you to triumph.
It is Christ who weathers the storm.
It is Christ who brings you through fire.
It is Christ who raises you above the flood.

No matter what you may face,
whether its death or divorce,
whether its loneliness or poverty,
whether its sadness or sorrow,
if you have been crucified with Christ, then you no longer live. These things can't destroy

someone who has died to them. None of these things hinder the work of the Lord. Not even death can stop Jesus from doing what He's going to do!

No, you can hold your head up, and strongly say: "Let me also go that I may die with Him."

When you get to the point where you would rather suffer and die than fail the Lord, He will do great and might things through you. When you overcome your objection to pain and your fear of rejection and death, the devil no longer has a hold over you. When you have more faith in God than you do in your circumstances, you disarm the devil. You knock all of his weapons out of his hands, and he is rendered powerless to harm you any longer. Hallelujah!

By embracing the cross of Christ, we crucify ourselves upon it. We give God permission to kill off everything in us that displeases and dishonors Him. Our carnal mind will be transformed to a spiritual mind. Our flesh will die so our spirit can live. The world will grow stale and cold while God's presence and power will fuel and excite us.

Let the cross do its work. Ask God to use it to burn all the dross out of your heart so that only pure and refined gold remains. It is painful, I assure you. It is never pleasant to die, believe me! But it is necessary and vital to your well-being and your growth as a Christian.

I know a lady who wanted to draw as close to God as she could. Her problem was her husband held her back. He claimed to be a believer but he didn't love God and mocked her for doing so.

She went on a pilgrimage to Israel. While there, the Lord spoke to her. He told her, "If you want to draw closer to me, I will have remove everything that keeps you at a distance."

She knew he was referring to her husband. She said, "I am willing, Lord. I love you more than anything."

Shortly after she returned home, her husband left her and filed for divorce. It was terribly painful for her and their children. She wept many nights and second-guessed every decision she made. In time, however, the divorce was final and her feelings changed.

"Though I felt as if I were dying, I also felt the Lord's presence through it all. Now, I am closer to Jesus than I have ever been. My kids are happier now because they see the change in me."

Dying to self, dying to a dream is never easy but it is the only way we can make room for the Lord to operate in our lives.

"Father, use the cross to kill anything that impedes my growth. Feed me as I partake of Your Word daily that I may grow stronger in You. Wash me with Your precious blood, and empower me by Your Holy Spirit. In Jesus' Name, I ask these things. Amen."

It is in death to self where we find the Lord of Life. Come! Let us go and die with Him!

CONCLUSION

I believe it is a sign of danger when the ministers in the pulpits of the church find anything and everything else to talk about on Sunday mornings besides the cross and the blood. I am not advocating that we speak exclusively to these topics every Sunday. But because the cross and the blood are so fundamental to our doctrine as Christians, it is absolutely imperative we speak on them regularly to educate our new believers as well as remind our older ones of their eternal significance. To fail to do so is to rob Christians of foundational knowledge of their chosen religion.

The cross is essential to our understanding as it is the key to Heaven's door. If there had been no cross, there would have been no debt paid for our sin. Had there been no cross, it would be up to us to atone for our wickedness before a holy God who will not look upon sin. The power of the cross to kill our mortality and thereby free us to live a holy life before the Lord must be taught and understood by all born-again believers.

Jesus' blood is the only agent in the world to cleanse us of our sins and free us from shame and guilt. Because He bled, died and rose again, we have salvation, baptism in the Holy Spirit, divine healing, spiritual gifts, deliverance from bondage and the promise of His return in the rapture of the Church. We must understand what the blood did, is doing and will continue to do on our behalf as we

". . . work out our salvation with fear and trembling." (Phil. 2:12) We must have faith in and be bold in applying the blood of Christ to our lives and our loved ones. It is the only power given to man from the hand of God to protect us and bring triumph in adversity.

A person equipped with the blood of Jesus and the cross of Calvary with the knowledge of how to apply them will live a successful, triumphant Christian life.

Ignorance of their existence and power cripples the believer and leaves them vulnerable to satanic and demonic attack.

I urge all believers everywhere to read this book, understand its message and share this teaching with as many people as you can. It will strengthen other believers and draw the lost to Christ.

BLESSING

May you find forgiveness for your sins
under the shed blood of Jesus,
and may you find release
through the work of the cross
in your soul.
Finding yourself walking in forgiveness
and freedom with God,
may you extend the same
to those around you forever.

ABOUT THE AUTHOR

Steven Galindo is a native Houstonian and has been involved in pastoral ministry for over 20 years. He is a graduate of Central Bible College in Springfield, MO. He is a preacher, teacher, writer, singer and counselor. He and his wife live in Joplin, Missouri. This is his 10th book.

To contact Steven Galindo, you may write him at stevengalindo61@gmail.com.

Or visit him at www.facebook.com/stevengalindo

For further reading on this subject –

Derek Prince – *Bought with Blood: The Divine Exchange at the Cross*

Andrew Murray – *The Blood of the Cross, and The Power of the Blood of Jesus*

Billye Brim – *The Blood and the Glory*

H. A. Maxwell Whyte – *The Power of the Blood*

Kenneth E. Hagin – *The Precious Blood of Jesus*

Turn the page for more books from Steven Galindo

The Healing Power of Forgiveness

    Are you troubled by past memories filled with shame and regret? Do you struggle with forgiving others for past hurts? Do you feel remorse and need to be forgiven?
    In The Healing Power of Forgiveness, author Steven Galindo discusses how to forgive others, how to forgive yourself and how to forgive God as well as how to ask for and receive forgiveness, and how to release the past so you can embrace your future.
    This is an excellent reference for therapists, counselors and anyone suffering inner pain and needing release. Walk out of bondage and into freedom. Release your pain and unlock your joy!

    Visit www.createspace.com/3582168 to purchase your copy now!

From a Pit to a Palace, From Prisoner to Prince: Lessons Learned from the Life of Joseph

Take a fact-filled journey through the life of Joseph, the ancient Hebrew patriarch, and learn some important lessons about:
- dreaming God's dreams
- finding your spiritual gifts
- defining the true meaning of success
- understanding your place in the Kingdom

Each chapter is followed with important Lessons Learned as well as Questions to Discuss, making it ideal for small group study or one-on-one counseling.

Visit www.createspace.com/3611234 to order your copy!

The Gift My Father Gave Me

At 17, Matthew discovers he has a biological father he has never met. He and his Dad board a bus and head to Eagle Pass to meet his mysterious uncle, Tio Antonio.

Along the journey we are told a wonderful story, and witness Matthew receive two gifts -- wealth from Tio Antonio, and an even more valuable one from his father.

He learns a very important lesson in life we all need to understand: what makes us rich is not what we have but who we are.

Go to www.createspace.com/3656654 to buy your copy now!

Healing Mercy, Healing Faith, Healing Grace and Healing Power

Four devotionals designed to inspire and encourage those struggling with illness. Each book offers 30 healing scriptures and a short commentary that will uplift and inform doctors, nurses, ministers, counselors and loved ones of the healing power of God.

Despite what some cynics and critics may think, God is still in the healing business, and He has a word of healing for you and your family members.

Order all four at www.createspace.com/3623374.

Encourage Me

Steven Galindo

Drawing upon 20 years of counseling experience, Steven Galindo explores:

- Keys to encouraging yourself
- Developing a ministry of encouragement
- Resisting the voice of discouragement so prevalent in our world today

Also included are four testimonies of people who through life-changing experiences found a way to cheer themselves and others.

This is an excellent resource for counselors, pastors and lay leaders who work with people struggling with stress, heartache and hopelessness.

Go to: www.createspace.com/3722549 for your copy now!

A Prescription for Peace

    The world is full of trials and difficulties. It is easy to lose your peace of mind and give in to worry, fear, doubt and anxiety.

    A Prescription for Peace is medicine from the Bible that restores tranquility to the troubled soul. Each page of this 30-page devotional offers a scripture, a commentary and a prayer designed to calm your nerves, encourage your heart and develop your peace of mind.

    This is a wonderful resource for counselors, pastors and chaplains working with struggling believers.

Get your copy at: www.createspace.com/4076096

Printed in Great Britain
by Amazon